Red Pepper Fudge
and
Blue Ribbon Biscuits

Red Pepper Fudge
and
Blue Ribbon Biscuits

Favorite Recipes and Stories
From North Carolina State Fair Winners

Amy Rogers

Illustrations by Warren Burgess

Photographs by the Author

 Down Home Press, Asheboro, N.C.

ISBN 1-878086-43-X

Library of Congress Number 95-069885

Printed in the United States of America

Book design by Elizabeth House

Cover Illustration by Warren Burgess

Down Home Press
P.O. Box 4126
Asheboro, N.C. 27204

To the memory of my parents,
Marshall and Elaine Rogers,
who taught me that good food
is reason enough to celebrate
and
to John,
who made me a Southerner

Acknowledgements

This book would not have been possible without the help and support of family, friends and co-workers — and the wonderful people who enter the North Carolina State Fair and make it a success every year.

I especially want to thank Nola Alderman of the State Fair, who saved me many miles of driving and hours of research by helping me locate winners. Wesley Wyatt assisted in my efforts to contact prior-year entrants.

I am grateful to my friends and co-workers at Little Professor Books in Charlotte. They supported me with their considerable good humor during the writing of this book.

My neighbors and friends cheerfully tasted and critiqued my amateur attempts at these first-rate recipes. Glenda Woolf rescued me from my repeated computer crashes. My thaks to Warren Burgess for his illustrations and friendship.

Julie Rogers, Adam Rogers and Mike Yonkovig knew more than anyone how much this project meant to me. My husband knew when to talk and when to listen: John, thank you for keeping me on the map.

I owe much to the good judgment of Jerry Bledsoe, who never doubted this idea was a good one, even when others did.

Most of all, I want to thank the State Fair winners whose stories are told here. For their kindness, warmth, patience and devotion to their craft, they deserve more recognition than this book can give them.

Contents

Introduction

It wasn't easy to find North Carolina's State Fair blue-ribbon-winning bakers. Over 3,000 miles and through the better part of a year, I searched them out in small towns, big cities and places I had to squint to find on a map.

Early in my quest, I learned that these were people who can't be categorized or compared like so many plates of buttermilk biscuits. Other than their love of cooking, there is no common trait that defines a State Fair blue-ribbon winner.

They are people who plant crops, practice law, work on assembly lines, care for children, run cash registers. Most are not boastful or eager to show off their considerable skills in the kitchen. They prefer cooking to talking about it.

Yet they opened their doors to me and shared their stories and the bounties of their expertise. In the best Southern style, they packed boxes with cookies and cakes for me to take home. They stuffed biscuits into bags, wrapped pies in foil and pressed them into my hands as I left.

I had thought that the gifts and secrets they were sharing with me had only to do with cooking, but I later realized they had as much to do with life.

For these exceptional people, cooking transcends the mere preparation of food. It links each family's past with the future, and it shows in their kitchens: handed-down recipes scribbled on scraps of paper; a hand-carved dough bowl worn smooth from generations of use; a dented bread pan that will someday be passed on to a child or grandchild.

For North Carolina's blue-ribbon winners, baking honors the best of family traditions.

The North Carolina State Fair

They come from miles around, bringing their best to the state capital each autumn. From champion beef cattle to delicate roses; from handmade quilts to bushels of corn; if it's grown or crafted by North Carolinians, you can see it at the State Fair. In 1994, nearly 700,000 people visited the Fair, making the ten-day exhibition the state's largest annual event.

A lot has changed since North Carolina's first State Fair was held back in 1853. A showcase for agriculture and manufacturing, it brought in an attendance of 4,000 or so, each visitor paying 25 cents — 50 cents for patrons arriving by buggy. With the success of that first undertaking, the stage was set for a tradition that would continue into the next century.

Gaining in popularity, the fair relocated each time the event outgrew its grounds. After World War II, entertainment became part of the roster of fair activities that drew increasing numbers of visitors.

Today, arts, crafts, trades and photography exhibits complement the livestock and agriculture contests. There are special categories to encourage children and young adults to learn the importance of healthy competition.

It will come as no surprise that food is as central to the State Fair as it is to North Carolinians' daily life. More than just cotton candy and corn dogs, the fair is a showcase for the state's best cooks and bakers. Judges must sample and evaluate the more than 1,000 culinary entries submitted each year before awarding their honors.

Though the North Carolina State Fair as we know it today is different from that of earlier times, much remains comfortably the same. Nowhere else is the pride that comes from the good, hard work of everyday life more visibly rewarded. The blue ribbon bestowed upon the top prize winner in each category is a tangible symbol of achievement. That honor is as meaningful today as it was in generations past.

Entering the Fair: Tips From Winners

DO follow recipes. Measure!

DO make several batches and enter only the best, most consistent samples.

DO read lots of new recipes to get ideas.

DO try to avoid baking when weather or humidity are unstable.

DO use fresh ingredients at room temperature, unless otherwise specified.

DO use "real" ingredients. Don't skimp and try to substitute butter blends or fat-free ingredients unless the recipe calls for them.

DO read instructions. You can be disqualified for the wrong size plate or number of items.

DO spend time learning to do it right. Even winners have occasional failures.

DON'T rush. Good baking requires patience.

DON'T make what you and your family don't like. If you don't enjoy eating it, you won't enjoy making it.

DON'T trust your oven's thermostat. Use a thermometer to obtain accurate results.

DON'T give up. Practice makes perfect.

DON'T depend too much on high-tech equipment. Nothing you trust a machine to do will turn out as well as something you "keep your hands in."

To Learn More About the Fair

Rules and categories for entering the State Fair are published annually. A division of the North Carolina Department of Agriculture, the State Fair administrative office is located at 1025 Blue Ridge Road, Raleigh, NC 27607.

About the Recipes

State Fair blue-ribbon winners have a simple philosophy. They bake what they like and they bake what works. They don't waste time and money just to impress people. Their recipes are extensions of the lives they live — approachable, filling, satisfying and real.

Each of the recipes in this book tells its own story. Some were handed down by word of mouth, others are new creations shared here for the first time. As a comprehensive study, this book is admittedly lacking. There are no chess pies, as much as North Carolinians love them, because no one could produce a recipe to compare with the best pie memory could recall. You won't find trendy concoctions either. They're just not popular with our state's best bakers.

What you will find are recipes that people enjoy. Cookies you can make with your family, cakes you can bring to a covered dish dinner and breads that will fill your kitchen with an indescribable aroma.

How These Recipes Were Tested

Before I wrote this book, I had never baked anything that didn't come out of a box. I believed that the ability to create cakes that melt in your mouth, or to coax bread into rising was inherited, not learnable. Baking was a mysterious ritual, performed only by the initiated who had learned their secrets years ago.

Then I discovered that women, men, kids, seniors, singles and married people, right here in North Carolina, were baking the best breads and most luscious desserts this side of a French patisserie.

Our State Fair blue-ribbon winners convinced me I could learn how, too. Step by step, these kind people revealed their hints, shortcuts and tricks. Generously sharing recipes that have belonged to their families, often for more years than anyone remembers, they steered me toward success.

Countless cakes, batches of brownies, dozens and dozens of cookies — every recipe in this book has been tested. Not by a chef in a restaurant or bakery, but in my own kitchen.

You can do it, too. There's something here for everyone, whether you're a first-time or life-long cook. Take your time, have fun and plan for the occasional surprise. As any other skill, once you learn the basics, each creation becomes your own.

About Equipment and Ingredients

Superlative baked goods can be produced with the simplest tools and ingredients. More important than a vast array of coated cookware or hard-to-find ingredients is the attention to detail a good cook learns to cultivate.

Some brief descriptions are included here to help define, for the uninitiated, the differences in the equipment and ingredients called for in these recipes.

Equipment

Saucepans: Fair winners recommend heavy stainless steel. Aluminum can react with some foods, causing discoloration, and glass pans often heat unevenly. A double-boiler insert is helpful to have on hand for melting ingredients such as chocolate.

Skillets: Stainless skillets are easy to clean, but nothing compares to a cast iron skillet. The key is seasoning the skillet properly before you use it. (See the story about Dee Pufpaff for instructions.) Never scour a cast iron skillet, and always dry it thoroughly after washing to prevent rusting.

Baking pans and sheets: Round, square and rectangular, there are more shapes and sizes than you can imagine. Most important is the finish. Dark non-stick coatings often make cookies, breads and cake crusts too dark. Glass baking pans produce inconsistent results in baked goods, but are fine for casseroles. Preferable are stainless or aluminum utensils. For cakes and pies, 8" or 9" pans are standard. Loaf pans are a must for baking bread. Consider buying a jelly roll pan for spreading candy; its edges keep things neat.

Bundt pans: With their fluted edges, they can turn a plain cake batter into an elegant-looking dessert. Newer pans with light-colored non-stick coatings are ideal for cakes that must bake a long time without overbrowning. Most hold 12 cups of batter.

Tube pans: Try to find one with a removable bottom, and "legs" for inverting the cake while cooling. The pan for baking angel food cakes, it's 9" or 10" in diameter.

Springform pans: Designed for cheesecakes, these are now available

in a variety of diameters, including individual serving sizes. The side
"ring" has a hinge that unhooks, releasing the ring from the bottom of
the pan. The baked cake is served without removing it from the pan
bottom.

Whisks, beaters and blenders: Each of these performs a specific
task. They are NOT interchangeable. Recipes in this book specify when
a certain utensil is required. (See Joanna Wolfe's Angel Food Cake
recipe for a description of the perfect flat whisk for whipping egg
whites.)

Pastry blenders: State Fair winners can tell by touch when a dough
feels right. None interviewed here felt this little wire gadget was
indispensable.

Mixing bowls: Slope- or straight-sided; metal, ceramic or glass; what
works best is a matter of personal taste. Invest in some larger-sized
bowls if you're going to try your hand at yeast bread. Dough can rise
unpredictably.

Mixers: These are the one concession to modern technology that
fair winners admit they like. Hand mixers are inexpensive; a free-
standing mixer with attachments is a real luxury. Helpful but not
required. Remember, almost any recipe here can be prepared using
only a wooden spoon, your hands, and effort.

Biscuit cutters: Blue-ribbon winner Virginia Jackson shapes her
biscuits by hand. But if you want to cut out your biscuits, use the metal
cutters designed specially to do the job. Do not use the rim of a
drinking glass; it will flatten the dough as you push down. Don't twist
the cutter; it will compress the biscuit's edges.

Cookie cutters: Not the same as biscuit cutters, these have narrower
edges and are designed for thinner cookie dough.

Cooling racks: Air must circulate under baked goods as they cool.
Buy several racks for cooling large batches of cookies.

Candy and oven thermometers: Indispensable. Loring Fishburne
tells us most oven temperatures are off the mark by 25 degrees or
more. An inexpensive oven thermometer can hang or sit on the rack.
For the most accurate reading, place it as close as possible to where the
pan will go. Margaret and Jennifer McLeod use only Taylor brand
candy thermometers; the tall, flat devices that clip to the side of the
pan. Another style looks like the round-headed meat thermometer; it's
also useful when dissolving yeast in recipes that specify a range of
temperatures.

Mixing and measuring spoons: You can't have too many.

Ingredients

Milk: Refers to whole milk, although lower-fat milk can usually be substituted easily.

Buttermilk: The critical ingredient in the southern buttermilk biscuit, buttermilk also can be used in recipes calling for sour milk.

Cream: Refers to light cream, unless whipping cream with its 40% milkfat is specified.

Evaporated milk: Used in confections, this whole milk has most of the moisture removed, leaving a higher concentration of milkfat.

Condensed milk: Often confused with evaporated milk, it also is concentrated but contains sugar.

Sour milk: Unpasteurized milk will sour naturally; commercially pasteurized milk won't. Unless you have access to unprocessed milk, use buttermilk in recipes calling for sour milk. As an alternative, make one cup of sour milk by placing one tablespoon lemon juice or white vinegar into a measuring cup. Fill to the one-cup mark with whole milk and stir well. (See Betty Reitzel's Irish Soda Bread or the Buie family's Chocolate Coffee Pound Cake.)

Butter: No substitutes accepted. Either salted or sweet as the recipe — or your personal preference — determines. Whipped butter cannot be used in baking.

Margarine: Can be substituted where indicated, as long as the brand you choose contains the required 80% fat that designates true margarine. All other spreads are just that: spreadable blends of fat, water, salt, coloring, flavoring and additives. Don't even think of using spreads in baking recipes.

Shortening: Loved and hated, these hydrogenated oils are indispensable to Southern cooking. They add volume and flakiness to baked goods and can sometimes provide a compromise between butter and lard.

Lard: If you don't want to know, don't ask. Both Virginia Jackson and Harvey Moser insist there's no substitute for this rendered pork fat in the perfect biscuit.

Oil: The varieties are endless. Differing in flavor, color and "smoking points," the wrong oil can ruin a recipe. Most baked goods that call for oil, such as Susan Moser's Pumpkin Walnut Pound Cake, do best with corn oil although safflower oil is popular, too. Never substitute oil in a recipe that uses butter.

Eggs: All recipes assume the use of eggs sold as "large."

Sugar: Unless specified, this means white granulated sugar.

Brown sugar: Either light or dark, both are flavored and colored with molasses.

Confectioners sugar, or powdered sugar: Finely powdered, it has cornstarch added to maintain its texture. Delicious for making frostings, don't substitute for granulated sugar in baking.

Honey: Substituting honey for sugar can be done, but it isn't easy, due to honey's density and concentrated sweetness. Wendy Hamby follows this rule: For 1 cup of sugar, use 3/4 cup honey and reduce total liquid in recipe by 1/4 cup. Add a pinch of baking soda. Don't use in recipes containing sour cream.

Corn syrup: A sugar pie lover's best friend. Irreplaceable when you need it, and difficult to substitute.

Baking powder: Most widely used is the double-acting type. Aluminum-free powders are available, but fair winners are loyal to the tried and true.

Baking soda: Used in recipes calling for sour milk or other acids. And don't use soda out of that box that's been in your refrigerator absorbing odors.

Salt: Iodized or plain is acceptable. You can cut back the amount called for if you're using salted butter. But omitting salt entirely can cause problems with rising.

Yeast: Either compressed in cakes or dry in packets, yeast is essential for bread-making. Most novices prefer the packets; no measuring, nothing to spoil. Experienced bakers like Linda Adams use only the compressed yeast in their recipes.

Baking chocolate: Unsweetened, it contains the cocoa "butter" and must be melted carefully, preferably in a double boiler.

Cocoa powder: Also unsweetened, with "butter" removed.

Chocolate chips: Milk, semi-sweet, light and dark, these are ready to eat or bake into recipes. Buy extra if kids are helping — more end up in their mouths than in the bowl.

Cornstarch: Best for thickening fruits containing acids, handle according to instructions to avoid a "raw" taste.

Cornmeal: Irreplaceable. Corn breads can't even be attempted without it. Check to see if your recipe calls for plain or self-rising. Comes in white, yellow — even blue.

All-purpose flour: A blend of hard and soft wheat, either bleached or unbleached. The texture will vary depending on where you live. In the South, softer wheat is favored for its reliability in producing light cakes and biscuits. In the North, hard wheat is the mainstay of kneaded breads.

Cake flour: Extra soft and lighter in texture than all-purpose.

Bread flour: Engineered to withstand the kneading bread requires.

Whole wheat flour: This is the culprit responsible for the brick-like breads cooks try once and then abandon. Most whole wheat flour is milled too coarsely to produce the texture fair winners demand. If you like the color and nutty taste, try to combine whole wheat with other flours. (See Cindy Rayno's recipes for some foolproof ideas.)

Self-rising flour: Containing salt and leavening, it can become unstable over time, and most Fair winners do without it.

Vanilla: Use real instead of artificial. You'll notice the difference.

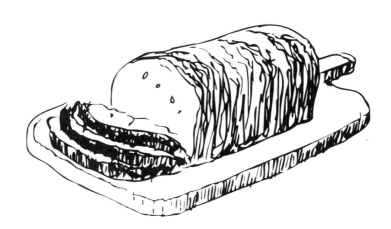

Raleigh

Margaret McLeod

"Cooking is easier, but I don't think it's any better than it was when I was growing up," Margaret McLeod says. And she should know. For more years than she can count, "Mama Mac" has been making the prize-winning cakes and candies her grandchildren finally convinced her to enter at the State Fair.

Her distinctive baking style developed early. She learned to cook, as many of the best cooks do, from her mother. One of eight children who grew up on her family's Durham-area farm, Margaret reminisces, "Daddy said if I slipped in the house and made biscuits, he'd know they were mine."

Today, Margaret and her neighbors at their Raleigh retirement community hold monthly fund-raising events called "Show and Sell."

"Some people even place 'orders' for my candy," she explains. "One man in our Sunday school class, he says, 'When I die, will you please put a few pieces of your fudge into my coffin?'"

It's no wonder. Attached to Margaret's multiple blue ribbons for fudge, divinity and cakes are such comments from the judges as, "Melts in your mouth," and, "Absolutely delicious!"

Granddaughter Jennifer shows every sign of having inherited Mama Mac's knack for candy-making. The 16-year-old is practicing the family fudge recipe, getting ready to enter her first State Fair.

Working together, these two generations of women are keeping alive some of their family's best traditions. Even William McLeod plays a crucial role in his wife's culinary success. "He does the shopping and the cleaning up," Mama Mac says with a smile.

But being known for making the best fudge can have its drawbacks, as Margaret learned when she was a student. "At Oak Grove School, back in about 1930," she says, "there was a boy who had his locker next to mine. He made a trip to my locker every day to see whether I had anything to eat. Anything that looked good to him, he'd take it."

She lowers her voice, puts her hands on her hips.

"So I made some fudge one time and I put Octagon soap in it! Red-hot pepper. Black pepper. I put everything I could find in there.

"The next morning, the teacher said we could go to our lockers when we finished studying. I said, 'Robert, bring me a book out of

Margaret McLeod and her granddaughter, Jennifer, cook up another batch of the fudge that made them famous.

mine.' But he saw the candy in there. He reached in and got him two pieces.

"When he came back up the aisle, he just opened his mouth and started spitting all over the floor. We had the biggest commotion that day you ever saw in your life!"

Margaret and her family soon moved to Raleigh, but some years later came back to Durham, where she found that her old schoolmate Robert lived just down the street. He was a good neighbor, she remembers, doing "a lot of little favors for our family." To thank him, Margaret sent her oldest son, Mac, to bring over some of her best fudge one day.

Robert opened the door. "Dang it, Mac," he said. "You eat a piece first!"

Jennifer McLeod

One recipe, one entry — and one blue ribbon for fudge. Now just 16 years old, Jennifer McLeod is off to a winning start.

She's the rising star of the McLeods — North Carolina's first family of fudge. Her grandmother, Margaret ("Mama Mac"), has given Jennifer both inspiration and insight. In a tough category, using a recipe that requires exact technique and timing, the youngest McLeod is already on her way to many more successes.

Like most teenagers, Jennifer stays busy. In addition to her schoolwork, her schedule includes drama, tennis and youth group activities, so she doesn't often have time to experiment in the kitchen. Her "pretty spicy" chili turns out well, but cookies have proven to be tricky. Luckily, Jennifer's friends are always willing to sample her recipes.

She makes fudge often. "About 15 or 20 batches in the last six months," she says. She doesn't worry about competition from her friends — none of them has expressed the slightest desire to challenge her.

"They're just happy to eat my fudge," she says with a laugh.

If there's anything unusual about Jennifer and Mama Mac, it may be the amount of time they spend together. These days, some families let their closeness slip away.

"We see each other at least three times a week," Jennifer says. "For dinner, or just to visit."

Entering the State Fair still feels new for this high school sophomore. Using the carefully chosen saucepan and candy thermometer her grandmother gave her, Jennifer is developing her own style.

Next, she plans to master Mama Mac's recipes for Divinity and Peanut Butter Balls. And if she's discovered anything at all that she doesn't like about cooking, she can sum it up easily in one sentence: "Doing the dishes."

Chocolate Fudge
by Margaret McLeod and Jennifer McLeod

       3   cups sugar
     1/2   cup Hershey's cocoa
     1/8   teaspoon salt
       1   tablespoon white corn syrup
   1 1/2   cups milk
     1/3   cup butter or margarine
       1   teaspoon vanilla
       1   cup chopped nuts

Butter a cookie sheet and set aside.

Mix together sugar, cocoa, salt, corn syrup and milk in a 4-quart saucepan. Over high heat, stir until mixture begins to boil. Clip candy thermometer to side of pan. Turn down heat to medium and cook without stirring until temperature on thermometer reaches 234 degrees.

Remove from heat. Add butter (or margarine) and vanilla. Do not stir. Let cool at room temperature for 15 minutes.

Beat with a wooden spoon only until fudge begins to lose some of its gloss and starts to thicken. Add nuts and quickly spread into prepared pan.

Cut into squares when cool. Store in an airtight container.

Yield: About 1 1/2 pounds

Hints

Be sure to use a pan large enough to prevent boiling over during cooking.

Mixture will boil quickly, but will take 20 to 25 minutes to reach 234 degrees. Margaret sets a timer for 20 minutes, then checks the temperature.

Do not stir after the mixture reaches boiling — it causes graininess.

In hot weather, you may want to allow an extra degree of temperature (235).

Don't overbeat. It makes the fudge too hard.

Red Pepper Fudge
by Margaret McLeod

This is the recipe that stops would-be candy thieves in their tracks. Although it would be a shame to waste a perfect batch of Margaret McLeod's chocolate fudge, if someone you know has been taking advantage of your cooking — and if you can handle the repercussions from playing a practical joke — here is what to do.

Follow preceding recipe for Margaret McLeod's prize-winning fudge. After you have cooked and beaten the fudge, but just before you spread it into the pan, add several (no need to measure) spoonfuls of:

Red pepper
Soap flakes
Black pepper

Stir to mix well, then spread into pan to cool. Use with caution!
Yield: More than anyone will want

Divinity Fudge
by Margaret McLeod

```
    1  cup white sugar
    1  cup brown sugar (NOT packed)
    4  tablespoons white corn syrup
1 1/2  cups hot water
    3  egg whites
    1  cup chopped nuts
    1  teaspoon vanilla
```

Combine both sugars, syrup and water. Dissolve thoroughly. Bring to a boil and cook mixture until a candy thermometer reaches 256 degrees.

Beat egg whites until stiff. Pour hot mixture over beaten egg whites, then beat with electric mixer for about 3 minutes. Add nuts and vanilla, then beat by hand with a wooden spoon until divinity loses its shine.

Drop by spoonfuls on wax paper immediately.
Yield: About 1 pound

Hints

Mrs. McLeod prefers Taylor brand candy thermometers.

Don't take your thermometer out of the hot pan and put it into the cold water in your sink! Let it cool to room temperature first.

Orange Pound Cake
by Margaret McLeod

1	cup shortening
1/2	stick butter
2 3/4	cups sugar
5	eggs
1	teaspoon vanilla
1	teaspoon orange flavoring
1	cup orange soda
3	cups all-purpose flour, sifted

Preheat oven to 350 degrees. Grease and flour a tube pan or bundt pan; set aside.

Cream together shortening, butter and sugar until light. Add eggs, one at a time, beating well after each addition. Add vanilla and orange flavoring. Then, alternately add the orange soda with the flour, ending with flour.

Turn batter into prepared pan. Bake for 1 hour and 10 minutes, or until a toothpick inserted comes out dry.

Let cool in pan 20 minutes or so before turning out onto a plate. Spread frosting while cake is still slightly warm.

Yield: 12 to 16 servings

Hints

Margaret uses Orange Crush brand soda.

Orange Frosting
by Margaret McLeod

    1/2   stick butter
      3   ounces cream cheese
      1   cup confectioners' sugar
      1   teaspoon orange flavoring
    1/2   teaspoon vanilla

Cream butter and cream cheese together. Add sugar and flavorings, and beat to spreading consistency.

Yield: About 1 cup

Cary

Cindy Rayno

There is nothing unusual about the house, nothing different about the neighborhood — or the cars in the driveway, or the kids playing in their yards. So what is it that makes Cindy Rayno a State Fair multiple blue-ribbon winner?

"I grew up baking," Cindy says, although she admits the first "mix" cake she attempted for her mother's birthday had to be held together with toothpicks. "I think I was nine or ten."

Watching Cindy make her famous cottage cheese rolls shows that success truly lies in the details. She makes a slight adjustment to the oven temperature, peeks at the dough to check its rising. (Some friends, missionaries from Nairobi, were due to arrive soon and the rolls had to be exactly right.)

Cindy thinks we've gotten away from knowing what it is that makes food good, makes it memorable. She shares this story: "I had made some of my cinnamon coffee rolls for church. A woman asked me, 'Couldn't I just make them with some frozen bread from the grocery store?'"

Cindy tried to discourage her.

"Well, she tried it anyway and said to me, 'That didn't work at all!'"

As with food, it's the details we so often remember about family, too; the smells from their kitchens, the sounds of their voices. Cindy recalls it all so clearly — one grandmother churning butter and the other making raspberry jam. She credits her mom's baking for inspiring her to excel.

"Mom's rolls, they would melt in your mouth — we always had them for Thanksgiving or Christmas."

Cindy lived in Illinois for just a few years, but it was long enough to meet her husband, Don. Though it might be easy to think of "up north" as big cities, traffic jams and bad weather, what Cindy remembers are cross-country skiing and hiking Illinois' Prairie Path. She and Don picked apples, blueberries and wild raspberries, and decided to try preserving and canning.   "I wanted to be a 'back to the basics' kind of person," she explains.

When a job for a chemist opened up in North Carolina for Don, the Raynos moved back to Cindy's home state. It wasn't long after that

Valerie and Amy Rayno are off to a good start. They've already won ribbons for baking with recipes learned from their prize-winning mom, Cindy.

that Don Rayno won the family's first State Fair blue ribbon — for some of those raspberry preserves.

Now living only about 50 miles from her family home in Mebane, Cindy is teaching her daughters Amy and Valerie the family traditions.

"They've cooked with me since they were old enough to sit up," she says. "Sometimes I'd even put the infant seat up on the kitchen counter to keep them near me. As soon as they were old enough, I taught them to crack eggs and measure ingredients. Now they like to cook on their own. Once they've made something a time or two they can do it without a lot of supervision."

In 1993, then nine-year-old Valerie won a ribbon for her biscuits, and the following year entered chocolate chip and sugar cookies, as well as a decorated cake. Younger sister Amy entered her banana bread, a family breakfast favorite.

Cindy has two shelves of cookbooks, but when asked to name her favorite source for recipes, she doesn't hesitate. *"Southern Living* magazine — and their cookbooks," she says emphatically.

Some foods have been part of people's families for so long that no one can remember where the recipes came from. Since their school days, both Cindy and her sister, Carolyn Wilson, who lives in Greenville, have been making Pepparkakor Ginger cookies.

"They've been around in our family for a long while," Cindy says. So have the sugar cookies and banana bread Amy and Valerie like to make from recipes handed down by Cindy's mom.

Asked why, in spite of her full and busy life, she enters the State Fair each year, Cindy smiles.

"For me, it's just for the pleasure of knowing I do something well."

Pineapple Cream Cheese Spread
by Cindy Rayno

     16 ounces cream cheese, softened
    1/2 cup crushed pineapple, drained
      4 tablespoons finely chopped pecans or walnuts
      2 teaspoons vanilla

Combine all ingredients and blend well. Cover tightly and store in refrigerator.

Yield: About 2 cups

Hint
Great served on banana or zucchini bread.

Blueberry Peach Pie
by Cindy Rayno

        1   cup sugar
        3   tablespoons cornstarch
      1/2   teaspoon cinnamon
        3   medium peaches, peeled and sliced (about 2 cups)
        2   cups fresh blueberries
        1   tablespoon lemon juice
        1   tablespoon margarine
            Pastry for double crust pie

Preheat oven to 425 degrees.

In a large bowl, combine sugar, cornstarch and cinnamon. Add peaches, blueberries and lemon juice. Toss to coat fruit.

Fit bottom crust into pie pan. Fill with fruit mixture. Dot with margarine. Cover with top crust, seal and flute edges. Make several steam vents with a sharp knife. Bake 15 minutes, reduce heat to 350 and bake 40 minutes more, or until crust is brown and filling is bubbly.

Yield: 8 to 12 servings

Cinnamon Coffee Rolls
by Cindy Rayno

1	pkg. dry yeast	1	cup margarine
1/4	cup warm water	1	cup milk, scalded & cooled to 110 deg.
4	cups flour	1/4	cup sugar
1/4	cup sugar	3/4	teaspoon cinnamon
1	teaspoon salt	2	tablespoons melted margarine
3	egg yolks,	1/4	cup pecans, chopped
	slightly beaten	1/4	cup raisins (optional)

The night before baking:

Sprinkle yeast over lukewarm water, stir to dissolve; set aside. Combine flour, 1/4 cup sugar and salt in mixing bowl. Mix well. Cut in 1 cup margarine with a pastry blender until mixture resembles cornmeal. Add yeast mixture, egg yolks and milk. Stir with a fork until well blended.

Cover with aluminum foil and refrigerate overnight.

The next morning:

Grease a 9x13" pan and set aside.

Combine 1/4 cup sugar and the cinnamon. Set aside. Roll dough on a floured surface into a rectangle measuring about 10x15". Brush with 2 tablespoons melted margarine. Sprinkle with sugar/cinnamon mixture, pecans and raisins. Starting at the wide end, roll up like a jelly roll. Pinch edges well to seal. Cut into 15 equal 1" slices. Place cut side down, equally spaced, in prepared pan. Cover and let rise in a warm place until doubled in size, about one hour. While rolls are rising, preheat oven to 375 degrees.

Bake for 20 to 25 minutes or until golden brown. While rolls are baking, prepare Vanilla Frosting. Remove from pan and cool on rack. Frost.

Yield: 15

Hints

These rolls are very impressive and not overly sweet.

Cindy prefers Fleischman's margarine to butter in these recipes.

To scald milk, heat just until bubbles begin to appear on the surface. Remove from heat and allow to cool.

Use a thermometer to check the temperature of the liquid. If it's too hot it will kill the yeast.

Cindy likes to use unbleached flour in her recipes.

Vanilla Frosting
by Cindy Rayno

1 1/2   cups confectioners' sugar
   2   tablespoons softened margarine
1 1/2   teaspoons vanilla
1 to 2   tablespoons hot water

Mix sugar and margarine. Add vanilla and 1 tablespoon hot water. Stir well until blended. Add more water, if needed, a few drops at a time until frosting is smooth enough to spread.

Yield: 1 to 1 1/2 cups

Fresh Apple Cake
by Cindy Rayno

2	cups sugar
1 1/4	cups vegetable oil
3	eggs, lightly beaten
2	teaspoons vanilla
2 1/2	cups flour
1	teaspoon baking soda
1/2	teaspoon salt
1	teaspoon cinnamon
3	cups apples, peeled and chopped
1	cup raisins
1	cup chopped pecans or walnuts

Preheat oven to 300 degrees. Grease and flour a tube pan; set aside. Mix sugar, oil, vanilla and eggs.

In a separate bowl, sift together flour, soda, salt and cinnamon. Blend dry ingredients with sugar mixture. Add apples, raisins and nuts. Bake in prepared pan for 1 hour and 15 minutes, or until a tester inserted into cake comes out clean.

Cool in pan for 15 minutes before removing. After cake has cooled, drizzle with your favorite glaze or frosting.

Yield: 12 to 16 servings

Hints

Extremely moist. Sweet enough to serve without frosting if you prefer.
Batter will be thick and may require a spatula to spread into pan.
Do not use red or yellow Delicious variety apples in this recipe.

Pepparkakor Ginger Cookies
by Cindy Rayno

```
  1    cup sugar
  1    cup light molasses
  1    cup margarine
  1    tablespoon ground ginger
  1    tablespoon baking soda
  2    eggs, beaten
4 1/2  cups all-purpose flour
  1/2  teaspoon salt
```

The night before baking the cookies:
In a large saucepan, heat together sugar, molasses, margarine and ginger. When the mixture comes to a boil, remove from heat and stir in baking soda. Cool until lukewarm. Stir in eggs.
Gradually mix in flour and salt. Chill dough overnight.

The next day:
Preheat oven to 375 degrees. Grease a cookie sheet and set aside.
Work with about 1/4 of the dough at a time. Keep remaining dough cool.
Flour your rolling pin and surface only as much as needed to keep cookies from sticking. Roll thinly and cut with floured cookie cutters into desired shapes. Bake 7 to 12 minutes, using less time for a chewier cookie and more for a crisper cookie.
Remove from oven and cool on a wire rack.
Yield: 4 to 5 dozen cookies

Hint
These can be frosted or decorated with your favorite icing.

Sugar Cookies
by Cindy Rayno

   2/3   cup shortening
   3/4   cup sugar
     1   teaspoon vanilla
     1   egg
     4   teaspoons milk
     2   cups sifted all-purpose flour
 1 1/2   teaspoons baking powder
   1/4   teaspoon salt

One hour before baking:
Cream together the shortening, sugar and vanilla. Add egg and beat until light and fluffy. Stir in milk.

Sift flour, baking powder and salt together, then blend into creamed mixture. Divide dough in half. Chill 1 hour.

To bake:
Preheat oven to 375 degrees. Grease a cookie sheet and set aside.

On a floured surface, roll dough to 1/8" thickness. Cut into desired shapes with cookie cutter. Bake 6 to 8 minutes, or until golden brown. Allow to cool slightly before removing from pan.

Yield: 2 to 2 1/2 dozen

Hints
This classic recipe is great for kids learning to bake for the first time. It doesn't call for fancy or expensive ingredients. The dough can take a good bit of handling, and the light color makes decorating the cookies fun.

Molasses Oatmeal Bread
by Cindy Rayno

2	packages dry yeast
1/2	cup warm water, about 110 degrees
2	cups + 2 tablespoons quick rolled oats
2	tablespoons shortening
2	cups boiling water
1/2	cup molasses
4	teaspoons salt
5 1/2-6	cups all-purpose flour
1	egg white, slightly beaten
1	tablespoon water

Grease 2 5x9" bread pans and set aside.

Dissolve yeast in warm water and set aside.

In a large bowl, place 2 cups of the rolled oats and the shortening. Pour in the boiling water and stir. Cool to lukewarm, about 10 minutes. Add dissolved yeast, molasses and salt.

By hand, stir in half the flour. Gradually add enough of the remaining flour to make a firm dough. Knead on a floured surface 5 to 8 minutes. Place in a greased bowl, turning to grease sides and top. Cover. Let rise in a warm place until doubled in size, about 1 hour.

Punch down dough. Divide in half. On a lightly floured surface, roll or pat each half into a 7x14" rectangle. Starting at the shorter end, roll up tightly, pressing with each motion. Pinch edges and ends to seal.

Place loaves in prepared pans, cover and let rise again until doubled in size, about 1 hour.

While dough is rising, preheat oven to 400 degrees. Blend egg and 1 tablespoon water. When dough has risen, brush tops of loaves with egg mixture. Sprinkle with remaining 2 tablespoons of rolled oats.

Bake 35 to 40 minutes or until golden brown. Remove from oven, turn out of pans and cool on wire racks.

Yield: 2 loaves

Whole Wheat Cottage Cheese Rolls
by Cindy Rayno

1 1/2-2	cups bread flour
2	cups whole wheat flour
2	packages dry yeast
1/4	cup packed brown sugar
2	teaspoons salt
1/2	teaspoon baking soda
1/2	cup water
1 1/2	cups (12-ounce carton) small curd cottage cheese
2	tablespoons margarine
2	eggs
	Melted butter or margarine to brush on top

Grease 3 muffin pans or 2 baking sheets and set aside.

In a large bowl, combine 3/4 cup of the bread flour, 3/4 cup of the whole wheat flour, yeast, brown sugar, salt and baking soda. Mix well.

In a saucepan, heat water, cottage cheese and margarine until warm, about 120 degrees. (Margarine does not need to melt.) Add to the flour mixture. Add eggs and blend at low mixer speed until moistened. Beat 3 minutes at medium speed or 5 minutes by hand.

By hand, gradually stir in remaining bread flour and enough of the whole wheat flour to make a firm dough. Knead on a floured surface until smooth and elastic, 5 to 8 minutes. Place in a greased bowl, turning to grease sides and top. Cover. Let rise in a warm place until doubled in size, about 1 hour.

Punch down dough. Divide into 6 equal parts. Divide each part into 6 equal pieces. Shape each piece into a smooth ball. Place in prepared pans. Cover. Let rise in a warm place until doubled in size, about 45 minutes.

While dough is rising, preheat oven to 375 degrees. When dough has risen, bake for 12 to 15 minutes. Remove from oven and brush with melted butter. Remove from pans to cool.

Yield: 3 dozen

Honey Whole Wheat Bread
by Cindy Rayno

3 1/2-4	cups all-purpose flour
2	1/2 cups whole wheat flour
2	packages dry yeast
1	tablespoon salt
1	cup milk
1	cup water
1/2	cup honey
3	tablespoons shortening
1	egg

Grease 2 5x9" bread pans. Set aside.

In a large bowl, combine 2 cups all-purpose flour, 1 cup whole wheat flour, yeast and salt. Mix well.

In a saucepan, heat milk, water, honey and shortening until warm, about 120 degrees. Shortening does not need to melt. Add to flour mixture, then add egg. Blend until moistened. Beat about 3 minutes on medium mixer speed or 5 minutes by hand.

By hand, gradually stir in remaining whole wheat flour and enough of the all-purpose flour to make a firm dough. Knead on a floured surface until smooth and elastic, 5 to 8 minutes. Place in a greased bowl, turning to grease sides and top. Cover. Let rise in a warm place until doubled in size, about 1 hour.

Punch down dough. Divide in half. On a lightly floured surface, roll or pat each half into a 7x14" rectangle. Starting at the shorter end, roll up tightly, pressing with each motion. Pinch edges and ends to seal.

Place loaves in prepared pans, cover and let rise again until doubled in size, about 30 to 40 minutes.

While dough is rising, preheat oven to 375 degrees. When dough has risen, place loaves in oven and bake 35 to 40 minutes or until golden brown. Remove from oven, turn loaves out of pans and cool.

Yield: 2 loaves.

Hint
Cindy likes Rapid-Rise brand yeast.

Quick Cream Cheese Crescent Rolls
by Cindy Rayno

    3   cups unbleached all-purpose flour
    1   tablespoon sugar
    1   teaspoon salt
  1/2   package dry yeast
  1/2   cup hot water, 125 to 130 degrees
    8   ounces cream cheese, softened
    1   egg
    1   tablespoon margarine or butter, melted
        Shallow pan of boiling water

Grease a baking sheet and set aside. Measure 1 cup of the flour and set aside.

In a large bowl, combine remaining flour, sugar, salt and yeast. Stir in hot water and cream cheese. Mix in egg and only enough of the reserved flour to make a soft dough.

On a floured surface, knead for 4 minutes. Divide dough in half. Roll each half into a circle about 10" in diameter. Cut each circle into 6 wedges. Beginning at the wide end of each wedge, roll up to the opposite end and pinch to seal the points.

Shape into crescents and place on baking sheet. Cover.

Remove pan of boiling water from heat. Set the baking sheet over the pan and let crescents rise for 25 to 30 minutes.

While dough is rising, preheat oven to 425 degrees. After dough has risen, place in oven and bake 10 to 12 minutes or until golden brown.

Remove from oven and brush with melted margarine or butter.

Yield: 12

Greensboro

Don and Becky Buie

Hard to imagine Don Buie as a sickly child, looking at him today. He's a big man, easily lifting his four-year-old daughter, Lauren, into the air.

"Daddy, I want to take the picture sitting on your shoulder," Lauren pleads. Her father obliges, and Lauren sits still just long enough for the shutter to snap.

He grew up in Red Springs in Cumberland County and remembers his mother calling him into the kitchen when he wasn't feeling well enough to play outdoors.

"I learned to bake from the time I was 12 or 13 years old," he says. "On a wood stove."

It was in school that Don met his wife. "I went to my first State Fair — with Becky — during my second year of law school. She had been to fairs back home in Tennessee, but I had always been sick when my class took their field trips to the Fair."

Once Don passed the bar exam, it wasn't difficult to convince Becky, also a lawyer, to make her home in North Carolina. "I like it here," she says, "the small cities, close together. People really have a lot of pride in the place they live."

The Buies lament the loss of part of their family heritage, because no one kept recipes. Eliza Buie never did write down the recipes her son uses today, but Don remembers her teaching him that "practice makes perfect" in baking.

Says Becky, wistfully, "My grandmother, Lucy Derrick, was just a 'natural' cook. She was famous at church for her pies. I try to make them, but it's just not the same. Her rolls would melt in your mouth, and we had always planned to make them together. But she took her recipe to her grave."

Nevertheless, Don and Becky began entering both the State Fair and the regional Dixie Classic Fair in the late 1980s. Competing was Becky's idea, since she thinks Don's cakes are "a step above" others. But Don jumped at the chance to get involved. Now, the Buies plan some extra time off when preparing their entries each year, and their co-workers tease them about catching "Fair Fever" when it comes time to get ready.

Lauren Buie, center, would rather be tasting cakes baked by prize-winning parents Becky and Don than posing for a picture.

The Buies handle the "two cooks, one kitchen" dilemma handily. Says Don, "When I'm in the kitchen she stays out. When she's in the kitchen, I stay out!"

But there are minor differences in each winner's approach.

As Becky explains, "I grew up using Crisco and flour on my baking pans. But Don doesn't do his that way. He believes in using wax paper."

Interesting to note that neither winner has had any success at all using the other's method.

Don devised an innovative solution when one of his chocolate pound cakes didn't turn out looking pretty enough. "I put frosting on it and it won second place," he says with a smile.

He misses the kind of cooking he grew up with, the kind that requires more time and patience than modern life allows.

"When I go home, my mother always cooks greens, field peas, macaroni and cheese, chicken and rice....."

"*MY* mother made the best biscuits," Becky interjects, "but Donald thinks *HIS* mother makes the best biscuits."

Both got their love of cooking from their mothers, and it is that love that leads them to enter the State Fair.

"It's the fun of participating," Don says. "You just have to enjoy what you're doing. Don't cook just to be cooking."

Becky adds, "If you're just 'going through the motions,' it's not going to turn out well. You have to want to be in the kitchen. You have to really like it yourself, then most other people will, too."

Lauren insists on having the last word. With a child's simplicity and honesty, she chimes in, "Everything we cook is a good idea."

Coconut Pound Cake
by Don and Becky Buie

2	sticks butter
2/3	cup shortening
3	cups sugar
5	eggs
3	cups flour
1	teaspoon baking powder
1	cup milk
2	teaspoons coconut flavoring
3 1/2	ounces flaked coconut

Preheat oven to 325 degrees. Grease and flour a tube or bundt pan. Set aside.

In a large bowl, combine the butter and shortening. Beat in sugar until fluffy. Add eggs, one at a time, mixing until well-blended.

In a small bowl, sift together the flour and baking powder. Add flour mixture, alternately with the milk, to the creamed ingredients. Stir in the coconut and flavoring.

Pour into prepared pan and bake 1 1/2 hours, or until a tester inserted into the center of cake comes out clean.

Cool on rack before inverting on plate to serve.

Yield: 12 to 16 servings

Chocolate-Coffee Pound Cake
by Don and Becky Buie

1 1/2	cups butter, softened
3	cups sugar
2	teaspoons vanilla
5	eggs
2	teaspoons instant coffee granules
1/4	cup hot water
2	cups unsifted all-purpose flour
3/4	cup cocoa powder
1	teaspoon salt
1/2	teaspoon baking powder
1	cup buttermilk or sour milk
	Confectioners' sugar for dusting

Preheat oven to 325 degrees. Grease and flour a tube pan or 12-cup bundt pan and set aside.

Cream butter, sugar and vanilla in a large bowl. Beat 5 minutes. Add eggs, one at a time, beating well after each addition.

Dissolve coffee granules in hot water. Set aside.

In a separate bowl, combine flour, cocoa, salt and baking powder.

In this order, add alternately to the creamed butter mixture:

the flour mixture,

the coffee mixture,

the milk.

Beat only until blended. Pour into prepared pan. Bake for 1 hour and 20 minutes or until a tester inserted into the center of cake comes out clean.

Remove from oven and cool 20 minutes in pan before inverting on plate to finish cooling.

Dust with confectioners sugar.

Yield: 12 to 16 servings

Hint

To make 1 cup sour milk, put 1 teaspoon vinegar in a measuring cup. Add milk to fill to 1 cup mark.

Clayton

Linda Adams

When she first learned she was going to give birth to twins, Linda Adams thought, *Good. Now I can stay home and cook all the time.*

Up till then Linda and her husband, Brian, had had "a lot of pizza nights." Their town, Clayton, is like many small towns — lots of friendly people, but few restaurants offering much variety.

With Diana and Robin keeping Mom at home, Linda, a former veterinary technician, saw an opportunity to really improve her culinary skills. Brian was glad. He grins, remembering his wife's first attempts at baking, back in their college days.

"Biscuits from a mix. They were so hard that when you dropped one on the floor, it wouldn't even crack!" he says, shaking his head.

Today Brian and Linda have a bright, new home a few miles from town. It's perfect for their energetic young family. There's lots of room for Linda's baking, gardening and Christmas ornament projects, all of which have won ribbons at the State Fair.

It was a neighbor who first suggested a little friendly cooking competition. "We both thought, *We can do this. It's easy,*" Linda says.

But it wasn't. Although she didn't win a single ribbon her first year entering baked goods, Linda was determined to improve — and she did, winning the very next year for her Victorian-style gingerbread house, complete with lights.

She emphasizes, "When you see 20 or 30 cakes in a category, you know you have to be really good. These are truly some of the best cooks in the state."

Also a proud gardener, Linda decided her roses were easily as pretty as those she'd seen at the fair. Last year, at the last moment, she plucked one of her just-bloomed flowers on her way to Raleigh.

When her neighbor called, Linda thought she was joking. The red rose had won "Best of Show."

Diana and Robin are lucky. Linda bakes weekly what her three-year-old daughters call "Mommy-bread."

"That's the kind that doesn't come out of a plastic bag," Mom explains.

For would-be bakers who may get discouraged, Linda offers a story of disaster that turned to triumph.

A bowl with steep sides helps Linda Adams' bread rise perfectly.

"In 1993, I was in the middle of making a pound cake. I had never made this one before. It was 10:30 at night, and I wasn't paying attention. I was tired and I stuck my spoon in the mixer.

"It locked up. Before I could turn it off, I smelled the burning oil. The mixer was gone.

"I had a batter with three more cups of flour to add."

Even when she discovered both of her neighbors' mixers had broken that same evening, she refused to give up. She just finished the cake by hand.

"We blew up three mixers that night!" she laughs.

But her pound cake won a red ribbon.

Linda has learned the judges appreciate originality. She remembers, "I got my first blue ribbon for my Dill Bread last year. When I checked my entry, they said, 'Oh, you got a blue ribbon for White Bread, Yeast.' I know people thought I was crazy. I got so excited."

Although she may have first entered the fair on a whim, Linda has grown into a serious competitor. She believes there's an element of luck in winning, but her hard work is what makes her one of the best.

"Everybody was looking at me when I won," she says, "So I just said, 'You don't realize how long I've tried to get that blue ribbon!'"

Apple Pie
by Linda Adams

The crust:
- 2 cups flour
- 2/3 cup shortening
- 1 teaspoon salt
- Ice water

The filling:
- 5 to 6 apples, peeled and sliced
- 1 cup sugar
- 1 1/2 teaspoons cinnamon
- 1/2 teaspoon nutmeg
- 1 tablespoon margarine

Preheat oven to 350 degrees. Grease a pie pan and set aside.

Mix flour, shortening and salt until crumbly. Do not overmix. Add ice water a little at a time until you can form dough into a ball. Divide in half. Roll one of the halves into a circle and fit into the pan. Reserve other half to make top crust.

Into the bottom crust, place the apples. Mix together the sugar, cinnamon and nutmeg, then sprinkle evenly over the apples. Dot with the margarine.

Roll out top crust and fit over pie. Seal edges and flute if desired.

Bake until brown, about 45 minutes to 1 hour.

Yield: 8 to 12 servings

Variation:

Omit the top crust, and add instead:

         1 cup flour
         1 cup brown sugar
    1 1/2 teaspoons cinnamon
      1/2 teaspoon nutmeg
      1/4 teaspoon salt
      1/3 cup butter or margarine, melted

Combine all ingredients and mix until crumbly. Spoon evenly over apples and bake as above.

Hint
Also delicious as a topping on peach or blueberry pie.

True Pound Cake
by Linda Adams

    3 cups sugar (sifted)
    3 sticks butter
    8 eggs
    3 cups cake flour (sift twice)

Preheat oven to 300 degrees. Grease and flour a tube pan or bundt pan. Set aside.

Cream together butter and sugar. Add eggs one at a time, beating after each addition. Add flour 1/2 cup at a time. Beat well after each addition.

Pour into prepared pan and bake for 1 hour and 15 minutes, or until a toothpick inserted in the center comes out clean.

Remove from oven and cool in pan slightly before inverting on plate to finish cooling.

Yield: 12 to 16 servings

Hints
NEVER substitute margarine (or "light" butter) for the butter in a pound cake.

Do not test cake for doneness until it has been baking at least 1 hour.

Dill Bread
by Linda Adams

          1 cup milk
          1 cup + 3/4 cup warm water
        1/2 cup sugar
          1 tablespoon salt
          2 packages dry yeast
        1/3 cup oil
          1 egg
      1 1/2 tablespoons dried dill weed
  or 4 1/2 tablespoons fresh dill weed
          1 tablespoon onion flakes
    6 to 8 cups bread flour

Spray 2 bread pans with baking spray and set aside.

Scald milk. Let cool and mix with 1 cup water. Add sugar and salt; dissolve and set aside. In a separate bowl, dissolve the yeast in the remaining 3/4 cup warm water. Set aside.

Add oil, egg, dill weed and onion flakes to the water/milk mixture, blending well. Add 3 cups of flour, then the yeast mixture. Stir. Keep adding flour till you have a soft dough.

Knead about 5 minutes, or until dough is smooth. Cover and let rise, in a warm place away from drafts, until doubled in size — about 1 hour. Punch down dough, cover, and let rise for 30 minutes.

Divide dough in half. Press out air bubbles. Place dough in prepared pans and shape into loaves. Cover with a lightweight cloth. Let rise again until doubled in size.

While dough is rising, preheat oven to 350 degrees.

Once dough has risen, bake for 30 to 40 minutes or until golden brown. Remove from oven and turn loaves out of pans to cool on rack.

Yield: 2 loaves

Linda Adams' Bread-baking Hints

Linda likes to use a stainless steel tall-sided bowl, rather than a slope-sided bowl, for mixing and letting bread dough rise. The shape of the bowl helps push the dough up.

Dish towels may be too heavy for draping on top of the bowl during rising. She uses dampened paper towels instead. Cheesecloth works, too

— and so does a lightweight cloth diaper!

Don't time the bread's rising by the clock. Time will vary according to the temperature and humidity. Instead, practice until you know when it looks right.

On a cold day, you can let dough rise in an oven heated to about 80 degrees. Make sure the oven is turned off before placing dough inside to rise.

Don't let the dough rise too fast, or at a temperature too high. The yeast may develop an "off," or bitter flavor.

Linda likes to use light-colored pans. She thinks dark-colored pans can make crusts too dark.

For biscuits, try using powdered buttermilk.

For waffles, try whipping the egg whites before blending.

Linda also likes to use refrigerated bulk yeast, rather than the pre-packaged.

An innkeeper from Rhode Island taught Linda a trick she claims has helped make her bread "foolproof." When you are dissolving yeast, stir it until there are no little clumps at all. Often, the amount of liquid given to dissolve the yeast isn't enough, and the mixture is too "goopy." Use the same total amount of liquid the recipe calls for, but:

Increase the amount of water you use to dissolve the yeast.
Decrease the remaining milk or water accordingly.

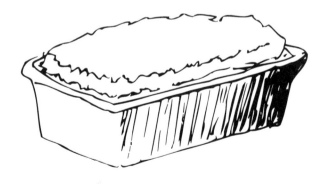

Davidson

Emily Barger

On a chilly gray Monday, welcoming aromas wafted from the farmhouse at the end of the long graveled driveway at the top of the hill.

Inside the large but cozy kitchen, junior division prize-winner Emily Barger was talking about the ribbons of several colors draped on the wooden cupboards and walls around her. Asked about any hints she might share with other cooks, she explained, "The Fair judges really look for uniformity in the culinary categories.

"Even though I've been baking since pre-school, some things just seem to turn out differently each time I make them, so I don't really have a secret I can pass along."

Discussing the finer points of fudge — and the tendency to overbeat or overboil it — Emily laughed.

"Sometimes I think that when I don't pay attention it turns out better!"

While some cooks hesitate to experiment with their families' treasured recipes, Emily and her mom, Brenda, like to vary the ingredients and techniques, customizing each recipe. "I'm working on a recipe for banana cupcakes — they're a good way to use up all those really mushy bananas," Emily said.

Seventeen-year-old Emily first started entering county fairs, as many students do, through a local 4-H club. One summer she taught younger 4-H kids how to make "bird bread." By learning to roll and tie the dough into the shape of a bird, kids develop the baking techniques that may help them become future prize-winners, too.

Are there any dishes Emily's tried that have failed? "Pancakes," she says emphatically. "Mine never, ever, turn out — no matter how many I make."

Brothers Jack and Sam, along with sister Kate, have all won their share of blue ribbons, too — "more ribbons than we can keep track of." Only Emily's dad, Hugh Barger, has never entered any of the fair's competitions.

"I started entering lambs when I was nine, but we've all four entered in that category," Emily says proudly, noting that lambs are one of the most competitive categories.

Emily Barger has good reason to smile. She's won ribbons for baking, sewing and livestock competitions.

But it was Emily's name that kept turning up on lists of winners in category after category, from livestock to baking to candy-making. And in 1993, she won the blue ribbon for a confection of a different kind — a floor-length red satin formal gown.

Walking outside to the misty pasture, Emily called her chestnut mare, Shadow, over to the fence. Her two dogs followed, close on her heels, as Emily thought out loud about the future.

"It's always fun to go to the Fair and see when you've won something — especially when you consider that you're competing with people from all across the state."

But next year, college will take Emily away from home, away from the place where she's already learned so much. "I hope Mom will cook for me then," she says with a smile.

Chocolate Pound Cake
by Emily Barger

      2 sticks margarine
    1/2 cup shortening
      3 cups sugar
      5 eggs
      3 cups cake flour
    1/2 teaspoon baking powder
    1/4 teaspoon salt
    1/2 cup cocoa powder
  1 1/4 cups milk
      1 teaspoon vanilla

Preheat oven to 325 degrees. Grease and flour a tube pan or bundt pan. Set aside.

Cream together margarine, shortening and sugar. Add eggs, one at a time, mixing well after each addition.

Measure and sift together the flour, baking powder, salt and cocoa. Add to creamed mixture alternately with milk. Add vanilla and mix well.

Pour into prepared pan. Bake for 1 hour and 35 minutes, or until cake pulls away from sides of pan.

Remove from oven and cool in pan at least 15 minutes before inverting to finish cooling on a plate.

Yield: 12 to 16 servings

Peanut Brittle
by Emily Barger

  1 1/2 teaspoons baking soda
      1 teaspoon water
      1 teaspoon vanilla extract
  1 1/2 cups white sugar
      1 cup water
      1 cup light corn syrup
      3 tablespoons butter
      1 pound shelled unroasted peanuts

Butter 2 cookie sheets and keep warm. Mix baking soda, 1 teaspoon water and vanilla, set aside.

Mix sugar, 1 cup water and corn syrup in 3-quart saucepan. Bring to a boil over medium heat. Cook, stirring occasionally, until mixture reaches 240 degrees on a candy thermometer. Stir in butter and peanuts. Cook, stirring constantly to prevent burning, to 300 degrees.

Immediately remove from heat. Stir in baking soda mixture.

Working quickly, pour half the candy mixture onto each cookie sheet, and spread to desired thickness (1/4 to 1/2" works best).

Cool, then break into pieces.

Yield: About 1 1/2 pounds

Hints

Stir the baking soda mixture briefly before adding it to the hot candy when you remove it from the heat. (It sometimes separates after you first mix it.)

Temperature rises at varying rates. It takes about 20 minutes to reach 240, then rises slowly to about 270. Watch out! After that, it reaches 300 quickly. Don't let the candy burn.

Banana Bread
by Emily Barger

```
1/2  cup shortening
  1  cup sugar
1/2  teaspoon salt
  2  eggs, beaten
  2  cups flour
  1  teaspoon baking soda
  3  large, ripe bananas, mashed
1/3  cup chopped nuts
```

Preheat oven to 350 degrees. Grease a loaf pan and set aside.

Blend together shortening, sugar, salt and eggs. Add flour and baking soda, bananas and nuts.

Bake for about 50 minutes, or until a toothpick inserted in the center comes out clean.

Yield: 1 loaf

Hint

This banana bread, like most, turns out best when baked in a metal loaf pan. Glass pans can make the crust too dark.

Banana Cupcakes
by Emily Barger

    1/2   cup shortening
      1   cup sugar
      1   egg, beaten
    1/4   cup buttermilk
  1 1/2   cups flour
    1/2   teaspoon salt
      1   teaspoon baking soda
      1   teaspoon vanilla
      2   very ripe bananas, mashed

Preheat oven to 350 degrees. Grease a muffin tin or place paper liners in each cup. Set aside.

Cream together shortening and sugar and set aside.

In a small bowl or measuring cup, beat together the egg and the buttermilk. Add to the creamed shortening mixture.

In a separate bowl, combine the flour, salt and baking soda, then add to the creamed mixture. Stir in vanilla and bananas; blend well. Pour into prepared tin, filling each cup about 3/4 full.

Bake for 20 to 30 minutes or until an inserted toothpick comes out clean.

Cool on a rack and frost with your favorite icing.

Yield: 12

Hints

Very easy to make. A good beginner project.

These look like muffins, but have a nice, cake-like texture.

Watch for overbrowning.

Lebkucken (Gingered Fruit Cookies)
by Emily Barger

```
  1   egg
3/4   cup packed brown sugar
1/2   cup honey
1/2   cup dark molasses
  3   tablespoons brandy
1/2   teaspoon grated lemon peel
  1   teaspoon lemon juice
  4   cups all-purpose flour
  1   teaspoon ground cinnamon
1/2   teaspoon baking soda
1/2   teaspoon ground cloves
1/2   teaspoon ground ginger
1/4   teaspoon ground cardamom
1/2   cup chopped almonds
1/2   cup finely chopped mixed candied fruits
```

Several hours before baking:
In a large mixing bowl, beat the egg and add the brown sugar. Beat until light. Stir in honey, molasses, brandy, lemon peel and lemon juice. Mix thoroughly.

In a separate bowl, mix together flour, cinnamon, baking soda, cloves, ginger and cardamom. Blend into molasses mixture. Stir in almonds and candied fruit.

Chill dough several hours.

To bake:
Preheat oven to 350 degrees. Lightly grease a cookie sheet and set aside.

Remove dough from refrigerator and divide in half. On a lightly floured surface, roll each half into a 9x14" rectangle. Cut into 2x3" rectangles. Place on prepared cookie sheet and bake about 12 minutes.

Remove from oven and allow to cool slightly before placing on rack to finish cooling. While cookies are still warm, brush with Lemon Glaze (next page) or your favorite icing.

Yield: 3 1/2 dozen

Lemon Glaze
by Emily Barger

    1   egg white, beaten
    1   tablespoon lemon juice
        Dash of salt
1 1/2   cups sifted confectioners' sugar

   Combine egg white, lemon juice and salt. Stir in confectioners' sugar.
Brush on cookies while still warm.

Hillsborough
Doug and Shari Vassello

The tomatoes were everywhere, even growing in the rose garden and out of the compost pile. Doug and Shari had wanted plenty — after all, Doug's family is Italian, and they love to make homemade spaghetti sauce. But the Vassellos didn't realize how tenacious North Carolina plants can be. So when the tomatoes threatened to take over their entire yard, the young couple knew it was time to get creative.

But a green tomato chocolate cake? And green tomato date bars? Well, the tomato IS a fruit....

Doug and Shari consider themselves lucky. In the 1980s, they were co-workers on the second shift at IBM in New York, fighting traffic and taxes, when they "saw the writing on the wall," Doug says. Layoffs were coming. Shari's father had been impressed by the people, the climate and the opportunities in North Carolina, so Doug and Shari requested a transfer. After waiting nearly a year, the newlyweds were ready to move south.

It took a while to feel settled, but IBM's moving coordinator helped make the transition easier. Even the family dogs, Ruff and Ready, had to adjust. It's all worked out well: Daughter Sarah was born in November of 1994.

Like lots of State Fair winners, the Vassellos have many talents. Shari's expertise shows in the needlework proudly displayed in their home. Both she and her husband make raspberry jam — from fruit that grows on plants they brought from New York.

"I challenged him to a 'jam off,'" Shari said, explaining how they got started entering the fair. (Doug won.)

Competing in the cookie category was Shari's idea, too. No one was more surprised than Doug when his oatmeal-raisin creations took the blue ribbon. Even his parents didn't believe it, since they have no family tradition of baking. Where Doug grew up, pastries came from a bakery, and families just made the coffee to serve along with them.

But what some people may lack in baking they make up for in cooking. Doug described the typical Vassello Thanksgiving dinner, Italian style: "First, there are all the appetizers — all kinds of pickles and olives and cheese. Then the lasagna or baked ziti. *THEN* the turkey and ham and all the fixings...."

A new home, a new baby and a blue-ribbon cookie recipe — Shari and Doug Vassello are putting down roots in North Carolina.

Doug and Shari have a unique approach to entering the fair. They learned the rules — about uniformity and color — but they don't believe you need to do a lot of planning or feel pressured. "We just pick out the six cookies that look the most alike and enter those," Doug said with a shrug.

They have fun making their now-famous cookies, buying different brands of ingredients and experimenting.

For a while Doug tried to make his recipe "semi-healthy." But the cookies came out flat and he couldn't figure out why. "This is not working," he remembered thinking.

So now he sums up the things he learned not to compromise on: "Big bittersweet chocolate chips. Two sticks of real butter and two eggs." (Not one egg or just the whites, he cautioned.)

"And when the recipe says, 'Nuts are optional,'" he instructs, "put in walnuts."

Oatmeal Raisin Cookies
by Doug Vassello

1 1/4	cups all-purpose flour
1	teaspoon baking soda
1/2	teaspoon salt
1/2	teaspoon cinnamon
2	sticks butter
1 1/4	cups firmly packed brown sugar (light or dark)
2	eggs
1/2	teaspoon vanilla
3	cups oats (not quick)
1	cup raisins or chopped prunes
1	cup crushed walnuts

Preheat oven to 350 degrees. Combine flour, soda, salt and cinnamon. Set aside.

In a separate bowl, beat butter and sugar until fluffy. Add eggs and vanilla; mix well. Blend in the flour mixture. Mix well.

Stir in oats, raisins (or prunes) and nuts. Batter will be thick. Drop by tablespoonfuls onto a greased cookie sheet.

Bake 10 minutes for a chewier cookie, 12 minutes for a crisper one. Remove from oven and cool on rack.

Yield: 5 to 6 dozen

Hints

Don't use a food processor to crush the nuts; it grinds them too finely. Instead, put nuts in a deep bowl and crush them with the bottom of a heavy glass.

Use two cookie sheets or wait until the one you are using has cooled between batches. Putting the dough on a warm sheet will make the cookies spread out too much.

If you like darker-colored cookies, use dark brown sugar. Light brown sugar will make a lighter-colored cookie.

Mystery Chocolate Cake
by Doug and Shari Vassello

2 1/2 cups all-purpose flour
1/2 cup cocoa
2 1/2 teaspoons baking powder
2 teaspoons baking soda
1 teaspoon salt
1 teaspoon cinnamon
3/4 cup butter
2 cups sugar
3 eggs
2 teaspoons vanilla
2 teaspoons grated orange peel
2 cups coarsely grated green tomatoes, stems removed
1 cup coarsely chopped walnuts (optional)
1 cup semi-sweet chocolate chips
1/2 cup milk
confectioners sugar for dusting

Preheat oven to 350 degrees. Grease and flour a 10" tube or bundt pan. Set aside.

Sift dry ingredients together in a bowl and set aside.

In a large bowl, beat together butter and sugar until smooth. Add eggs one at a time and beat well after each addition. With a wooden spoon stir in vanilla, orange peel and tomatoes.

Stir the nuts and the chocolate chips into the sifted dry ingredients. Add to the tomato mixture alternately with the milk. Pour batter into prepared pan and bake about 1 hour, or until a tester inserted into the center comes out clean. Cool in pan 15 minutes, turn out onto a wire rack.

Sprinkle with confectioners sugar before serving.

Yield: 12 to 16 servings

Hints

This cake keeps well in refrigerator without becoming dry.

Good way to use up end-of-season tomatoes that haven't had time to ripen.

Raleigh
Mary Richardson

Fear. It can stop almost anyone from taking a chance, from trying something new. Mary Richardson knows first-hand how fear changes lives. She listened to the words the doctor said, but all she heard was one thing.

She had cancer.

It was seven years ago when she got the diagnosis. "When you think 'cancer,' you think 'death,'" Mary said quietly.

"I remember going to the mall with my husband, Bill, shopping for a nightgown to wear in the hospital. I heard people all around me saying, 'Next month I'm going to do this or that,' or 'Next week I'm going here.'

"Plans. Everyone around me was making plans.

"I stood there and just thought for a minute, *There may not be a tomorrow for me. This could be the end of my life.*"

The surgery took place in September, and the doctors sent Mary home to mend. "I couldn't drive and I was bored out of my mind," she said. Then a friend suggested Mary try entering the State Fair, a few weeks away in October. She remembered thinking, *You know, I think I'll do that — just for fun.*

But it wasn't easy. Mary's incision made it impossible for her to stand up straight. "I bent over the stove to beat bread and make dough," she said. "I had no idea I'd win."

Over a plate of fresh-baked gingersnaps with strawberry cream cheese, Mary said, "Baking is a science." Her recently-remodeled kitchen boasts a six-burner restaurant gas stove and a pantry full of professional cookware — the Magic Line brand Mary prefers. She doesn't guess at measurements, and she always buys her favorite brands: Crisco and White Lily.

Mary's recipes are always in demand: Her cheesecakes are so sought-after that a businessman is considering buying one of her recipes. She tried her hand at catering, but found the workload overwhelming without a staff to assist her.

During the remodeling, Mary wasn't afraid to get her hands dirty outside the kitchen, either. "I ripped off the old mouldings and baseboards, then I went to the lumberyard, picked out new ones. Then

A newly remodeled kitchen, complete with restaurant stove, inspires Mary Richardson's scrumptious desserts.

I primed and painted them all," she said, then laughed, "I thought, 'Maybe I'm trying to do *TOO* much.'"

Life's lessons come sometimes, "through the back door," Mary believes. "Once you go through something like this, it gives you a certain urgency about life. It gives you a reason to plan and have goals."

So each year, right after the Thanksgiving dishes are washed and put away, Mary begins to prepare for the Richardsons' Christmas Open House. In a strange way, she's grateful things happened the way they did. "I really learned a lot — about faith, about God, about trust. And I learned a lot about myself," Mary said. "And other people."

She knows what matters: "Life is precious. Don't get discouraged."

Chocolate Caramel Cheesecake
by Mary Richardson

The crust:
  1 2/3 cups graham cracker crumbs
     5 tablespoons margarine, melted

  Preheat oven to 325 degrees.
  Combine crumbs and margarine and blend well. Press into a 9"
springform pan, using the back of a spoon. Bake for 5 minutes and
remove from oven.

The filling:
  14 oz. bag of caramel candies, unwrapped
   5 oz. can evaporated milk
      1 cup pecans, toasted and chopped
     16 ounces cream cheese, softened
    1/2 cup sugar
      1 teaspoon vanilla
      2 eggs
      1 cup semi-sweet chocolate bits or pieces, melted

  In a 2-quart saucepan, melt caramels and evaporated milk together
over low heat. Stir frequently until smooth. Pour mixture over crust. Top
evenly with pecans.
  In a bowl, combine cream cheese, sugar and vanilla, mixing until well-
blended. Beat in eggs.
  Add the melted chocolate and blend thoroughly. Pour into pan.

  Bake for 35 to 40 minutes. Remove from oven and cool several hours
in refrigerator to allow cake to "set." Do not remove springform sides until
cool.
  Yield: 12 to 16 servings

Praline Passion
by Mary Richardson

2	sticks margarine, melted
1 1/2	cups all-purpose flour
1/2	cup brown sugar, packed
1	cup oats
1 1/2-2	cups coarsely broken pecans
12 oz.	jar of caramel or butterscotch topping
1	can condensed milk
8	ounces cream cheese, softened
12	ounces frozen whipped topping

Preheat oven to 350 degrees.

Combine margarine, flour, brown sugar, oats and pecans and mix well. Spread evenly into a large cookie sheet (with edges). Bake for 20 minutes or until golden brown. Remove from oven and allow to cool, then crumble into pieces.

Put half the pieces into a 9x13" baking dish. Drizzle with half of the caramel topping. Set remaining crumb mixture and topping aside.

In another bowl, blend the condensed milk, cream cheese and whipped topping until smooth. Spread over the crumb mixture in the dish.

Top with remaining crumb mixture, then the remaining caramel. Freeze until ready to serve.

Yield: 12 to 16 servings

Gingersnaps
by Mary Richardson

       1   cup sugar
     3/4   cup shortening
     1/4   cup molasses
       2   cups all-purpose flour
       1   egg
       2   teaspoons baking soda
     1/4   teaspoon salt
     1/2   teaspoon cinnamon
     1/4   teaspoon ground cloves
       1   teaspoon ground ginger
           Sugar for rolling

Preheat oven to 375 degrees. Lightly grease a cookie sheet with shortening and set aside.

In a large mixing bowl, combine sugar, shortening, molasses and egg. Blend well. Stir in remaining ingredients by hand, or on lowest mixer speed. Mix only until ingredients are well-incorporated.

Form dough into balls about 1" in diameter. Roll in sugar and place on cookie sheet about 2" apart. Bake for 9 to 10 minutes. Remove from oven and allow to cool on pan for 1 minute; then remove to wire rack.

Yield: About 5 dozen cookies

Hints

Mary uses a restaurant scoop to make the cookies uniform in size.

Make sure your cookie sheet has cooled between batches — if you place dough on a sheet that is still warm, the dough will melt and spread out too far.

Mary serves these with strawberry cream cheese.

Caramel-Filled Cookies
by Mary Richardson

2/3	cup sugar	1/8	teaspoon salt
1	stick butter or margarine	1	cup pecans, finely chopped
1	egg, separated	12-15	caramel candies, unwrapped
2	tablespoons milk	3	tablespoons whipping cream
1	teaspoon vanilla	1/2	cup chocolate chips
1	cup all-purpose flour	1	teaspoon shortening
1/3	cup cocoa powder		

One hour before baking:

In a medium sized bowl combine sugar, butter, egg yolk, milk and vanilla. Beat until well-blended.

In a separate bowl, stir together the flour, cocoa and salt. Gently blend into the butter mixture. Chill dough in refrigerator for 1 hour, or until firm enough to handle.

While dough is chilling, very lightly grease two cookie sheets with butter or margarine; do not use oil. Set aside.

To bake cookies:

When ready to bake, preheat oven to 350 degrees. Beat egg white with a fork until frothy. Set aside.

Remove dough from refrigerator. Shape into balls 1" in diameter. Dip each into egg white, then roll in chopped pecans, coating well. Place on prepared cookie sheet about 2" apart. Gently press thumb into the center of each cookie, making an indentation about 1/2" deep. Bake for 10 to 12 minutes.

To make caramel filling:

While cookies are baking, melt together the caramel candies and the whipping cream in a small saucepan over low heat. Stir constantly until smooth.

Immediately upon removing cookies from oven, carefully press thumb into indentation again. Fill each indentation with caramel filling. Very carefully remove cookies with spatula and place on wire rack to cool. Set rack on wax paper.

To make chocolate drizzle:

In a small microwave bowl, combine chocolate chips and shortening. Heat on "high" for 1 minute. Remove from oven and stir until smooth, OR heat in the top of a double-boiler until almost melted; remove from heat and stir to complete melting.

While cookies are cooling on rack, drizzle with melted chocolate. Once chocolate has set, store cookies in an airtight container.

Yield: About 30

Hints

Place wax paper between layers of cookies when storing.

A sampling of the hundreds of baked goods submitted each year at the North Carolina State Fair.

Statesville

Loring Fishburne

"You see that?" Loring Fishburne is measuring his oven. "The opening is 18 inches high. The top of your cake pan should be exactly in the center of the oven.

"But if you put the rack on the middle level, the top of the cake will get too brown before the inside is done." He moves the rack down one level.

The retired lumber salesman and grandfather has been baking for about 15 years. Loring remembers, "One Christmas I told my wife, Ellen, 'Make me one of those sour cream-walnut cakes to take to a customer.' She said, 'You make it. I'll help you.'"

That cake started it all. After entering several local fairs ("Like shooting ducks in a pond," Loring says with a grin), he was ready to try his hand at the State Fair. Out of four entries he won two blue ribbons and a red.

But he acknowledges the changing tastes of some of the judges. "'Good flavor, but a little underbaked,'" he reads from one comment card, shaking his head. "But it's the same cake that won the year before."

No matter. Loring's cakes are famous. Take the one he contributed to a March of Dimes fund-raiser. He chuckles, "It was $1.50 a slice for 26 slices. One woman bought the entire thing and was happy to pay the $39.00!"

Loring likes to use yogurt or sour cream to make his cakes smoother. He bakes at least a dozen each month, and keeps a loose-leaf notebook of ideas, along with his own critiques.

He points outside, near the goldfinch feeder to two plain-looking sticks attached at one end to the house. He explains, "They're 'weather sticks' from Vermont. When the sticks point down, you might as well forget about baking." As if to demonstrate, the sticks droop down as wet snowflakes splatter on the Fishburnes' backyard deck.

Loring emphasizes the importance of following directions. "People would be surprised how well things turn out if they would only read the instruction books that came with their appliances." In the back of his notebook, he flips to two manuals. "The Whirlpool Stove and Oven Guide tells you exactly how to position your oven racks and pans."

Loring Fishburne's kids custom-made this apron for their family champion cake-baker to show off.

Then he reads aloud from the Sunbeam Mixer Guide, under "Better Cakes": "...beat until light and fluffy, about six to seven minutes." He even uses a timer to make sure he doesn't skimp on the mixing.

"It's a long time. But who does it?" He answers his own question. "Loring does."

But he learned one lesson the hard way. The first time he tried to enter the State Fair there was a problem. Loring baked a bunch of cakes, sliced them up, arranged them nicely on a big tray, and drove to Raleigh. They turned him away at the door. It seems Loring had failed to heed his own advice about following the rules.

"I didn't have an entry book to register like you're supposed to," he says. "But the lady there said, 'Those are the best-looking cakes I've ever seen. Come back next time.'"

Now he knows. "Nine out of ten people never look at the directions. Most don't even have them anymore. They've thrown away the rules just because they think they know how to turn the oven on!"

Success? "It's in the directions. All the basic things you need to know are there."

Chocolate Sour Cream Pound Cake by Loring Fishburne

2 sticks butter or margarine
1/4 cup vegetable shortening
3 cups sugar
6 large eggs
3 cups all-purpose flour
1/2 teaspoon salt
1/4 cup cocoa
1/4 teaspoon baking soda
1 cup sour cream
1 teaspoon vanilla

Preheat oven to 325 degrees. Grease and flour a 12-cup bundt pan. Set aside.

Bring all ingredients to room temperature. Cream together the butter (or margarine) and shortening. Gradually add sugar, beating until light and fluffy. Add eggs, one at a time, beating well after each addition.

In another bowl, combine and mix well the flour, salt, cocoa and baking soda. Add to the butter mixture, alternately with the sour cream, beginning and ending with the flour. Stir in vanilla.

Pour batter into prepared pan. Bake for 1 hour and 15 minutes, or until a tester inserted into the center of cake comes out clean.

Remove from oven and let cool on rack 10 minutes. Turn pan upside down on rack to remove.

Yield: 12 to 16 servings

Hints

Remember Loring's tip about placing the cake in the center of the oven; this really works well if you use a light-colored pan. Otherwise, the cake may get too brown.

Do not use baking powder in cake recipes calling for sour cream!

Lemon Yogurt Poppyseed Pound Cake
by Loring Fishburne

      2 sticks butter or margarine
    1/4 cup vegetable shortening
      3 cups sugar
      5 large eggs
      3 cups all-purpose flour
    1/2 teaspoon salt
    1/4 teaspoon baking powder
      1 cup lemon yogurt
      1 tablespoon lemon extract
      1 tablespoon poppyseeds

Preheat oven to 325 degrees. Grease and flour a 12-cup bundt pan. Set aside.

Bring all ingredients to room temperature. Cream together butter (or margarine) and shortening, adding sugar gradually until light and fluffy. Blend in eggs, one at a time, beating well after each addition.

In a separate bowl, combine flour, salt and baking powder. Blend the flour into the butter mixture alternately with the sour cream, beginning and ending with the flour. Stir in the lemon extract and poppyseeds.

Pour into prepared pan and bake for 1 hour and 10 minutes, or until a tester inserted into the center of cake comes out clean.

Remove from oven and let cool on rack 10 minutes. Turn pan upside down on rack to remove.

Yield: 12 to 16 servings

Hints

Remember Loring's tip about placing the cake in the center of the oven; this really works well if you use a light-colored pan. Otherwise, the cake may get too brown.

Do not use baking soda in cake recipes calling for yogurt.

Peaches and Cream Pound Cake
by Loring Fishburne

2	sticks butter or margarine
1/4	cup vegetable shortening
3	cups sugar
5	large eggs
3	cups all-purpose flour
1/2	teaspoon salt
1/4	teaspoon baking soda
1	cup sour cream
1	cup peaches, peeled and mashed
1/4	cup peach liqueur
1	teaspoon vanilla

Preheat oven to 325 degrees. Grease and flour a 12-cup bundt pan. Set aside.

Bring all ingredients to room temperature.

In a large bowl, cream together the butter (or margarine) and shortening. Gradually add sugar, beating until light and fluffy. Add eggs, one at a time, beating well after each addition.

In another bowl, mix together the flour, salt and baking soda. Add to the butter mixture, alternating with the sour cream, beginning and ending with the flour. In a small bowl, combine the peaches, vanilla and liqueur. Fold peach mixture into the batter.

Pour into prepared pan. Bake for 1 hour and 10 minutes, or until a tester inserted into the center of cake comes out clean.

Remove from oven and let cool on rack 10 minutes. Turn pan upside down on rack to remove.

Yield: 12 to 16 servings

Hints

Remember Loring's tip about placing the cake in the center of the oven; this really works well if you use a light-colored pan. Otherwise, the cake may get too brown.

Do not use baking powder in cakes recipes calling for sour cream!

Raleigh

Bobbie Bailey

It's quiet now at Bobbie Bailey's house. Daughter Renee has grown up and married, moved out on her own. Husband Floyd is taking it easy since his heart surgery. But Bobbie isn't slowing down.

"Once you've won your first ribbon, you can hardly wait for the next year," the Raleigh native says. It's early March and Bobbie has been busy. She's already planted flowers around the mailbox, hung the St. Patrick's Day decorations (and put on a green blouse to match), and picked out two recipes she wants to enter at the State Fair next October.

"I have entered pound cake every year and have never won," she says, describing a highly competitive category. Last year, one of the judges found Bobbie's entry lacking in texture. So next time, Bobbie plans to enter a cake from a cookbook she got when she and Floyd were newlyweds. The recipe calls for ten eggs. "Whipping those ten eggs whites will surely give that cake some texture," she promises.

In spite of her failure to capture the blue ribbon for pound cake yet, Bobbie has been successful in other categories. She has won for biscuits, a contest even lifelong winners admit is one of the hardest to win. Her pear relish won its first time, and Bobbie's the proud recipient of dozens of ribbons in every color, many for horticulture.

Her mother and grandmother loved flowers, and Bobbie knows there's something wonderful about gardening. "It's good therapy. You forget your aches and pains," she says with a smile.

Preparing culinary entries for the fair can be exhausting and hectic, especially if you enter the separate contests sponsored by Land-O-Lakes butter or Soft-as-Silk flour or the Egg Board. Bobbie enters them all. She admits, "Sometimes Floyd says he wishes I'd hang up my cooking and just enter flowers."

She loves to grow and cook vegetables. "Turnip greens and turnips, collards, green beans, cabbage — and sweet potatoes, butter beans, peas, corn. I'll make three or four a night. But I cook them the old-fashioned way. I don't put them on and let them stay five minutes. I put them on and let them stay two hours!"

Bobbie's been known to make more than 40 loaves of bread at Christmas time — without a bread machine — for gifts. Like most fair

Flowers and food
— Bobbie Bailey's
State Fair ribbons
cover her kitchen
table.

winners, she's not impressed with high-tech kitchen gadgets. She's never taken a cooking class.

Perhaps it's Bobbie's memory that helps her excel. She remembers many years back, before the state built Highway 70 and all around was farmland. Back when the roads at the fair weren't paved and a rainstorm would turn the grounds to mud. Times may have changed, but good cooking hasn't. If simplicity is part of success, Bobbie Bailey is happy to share her secret: "Old-fashioned ingredients. Self-rising flour, Crisco and buttermilk."

Coconut-Chocolate Bars
by Bobbie Bailey

12 oz. shredded coconut
    1 box confectioners' sugar
    1 can condensed milk
    1 cup pecans (optional)
    1 package of candy melts

Combine all ingredients except chocolate and form into bars. Let sit for 2 hours.

Melt chocolate according to package instructions. Dip bars into chocolate and place on wax paper to cool.

Store in refrigerator.

Yield: About 2 dozen

Hint
Candy melts can be found at craft stores selling candy-making supplies.

Million Dollar Caramel Nut Candies
by Bobbie Bailey

14 oz. bag of caramel candies, wrappers removed
3 to 4 tablespoons milk
    2 cups broken pecans
    1 bag candy melts

Melt caramels and milk together in a saucepan over low heat. Add pecans. Drop by teaspoon onto greased waxed paper. Chill for several hours.

Melt candy melts in a heavy pan over low heat according to package instructions.

Dip chilled candies in melted chocolate and place on wax paper to cool. Store in refrigerator.

Yield: About 3 dozen

Hint
Candy melts can be bought at candy-making and craft supply stores.

Sour Cream Apple Squares
by Bobbie Bailey

        2   cups all purpose flour
      1/2   cup butter or margarine, softened
        2   cups firmly packed light brown sugar
        1   cup chopped nuts
        2   teaspoons cinnamon
        1   teaspoon baking soda
        1   teaspoon salt
        1   cup sour cream
        1   teaspoon vanilla
        1   egg
        2   cups peeled, finely chopped apples (about 2)

Preheat oven to 350 degrees.

Blend together flour, butter and sugar until crumbly. Stir in nuts. Press 2 3/4 cups of this mixture into an ungreased 9x13" pan.

To remaining mixture add cinnamon, soda, salt, sour cream, vanilla and egg. Blend well. Stir in apples. Spoon evenly over base. Bake 30 to 40 minutes until a toothpick inserted in the center comes out clean. Cut into squares.

Yield: 18 to 24 squares

Sweet Potato Pie
by Bobbie Bailey

        1   heaping cup of sweet potato, cooked and mashed
        1   stick butter, melted
    2 1/2   cups sugar
        1   teaspoon baking powder
        4   eggs
      2/3   cup milk
        1   teaspoon vanilla
      1/2   teaspoon nutmeg, optional
        1   unbaked pie shell

Preheat oven to 400 degrees.

In a mixing bowl, blend together the cooked sweet potato, melted butter and sugar. Beat in the baking powder, then the eggs.

Stir in the milk, vanilla and nutmeg. Pour into pie shell. Bake for 10 minutes at 400 degrees, then lower the temperature to 325 degrees and bake for 30 minutes.

Yield: 6 to 8 servings

Lemon Bread
by Bobbie Bailey

1 1/4   cups sugar
   6   tablespoons shortening
   1   tablespoon grated lemon rind
   2   eggs
1 1/2   cups sifted all-purpose flour
 1/2   teaspoon salt
   1   teaspoon baking powder
 1/2   cup milk
 1/2   cup chopped nuts
     Juice of 1 lemon (about 3 tablespoons)

Preheat oven to 325 degrees. Grease a 5x9" loaf pan and set aside.

In a medium-size mixing bowl, cream together 1 cup of the sugar and the shortening. Add lemon rind and beat in eggs.

In a separate bowl, sift together flour, salt and baking powder. Add to the creamed mixture alternately with the milk, beginning and ending with the flour. Stir in nuts.

Pour into prepared pan. Bake 40 to 50 minutes, or until a tester inserted into the center comes out clean.

While bread is baking, combine the lemon juice and the remaining 1/4 cup sugar in a small saucepan. Heat and stir until dissolved.

When bread has finished baking, remove from oven. Pour lemon juice glaze over hot bread. Allow to cool completely in pan before removing.

Yield: 1 loaf

Raleigh

Kris Harris

It began when she was a little girl, after she read about the pioneers in *Farmer Boy*, one of the Little House on the Prairie books. That was when Kris Harris knew she wanted to learn about sewing, quilting, cooking and baking.

"I read about how the family would enter their big pumpkins in the county fair, and that got me started," Kris reminisced.

She began baking at age eight and first entered New York's Dutchess County Fair at age 14.

A native of Wappingers Falls, New York, Kris originally planned to work in forestry. She met her husband, Dave, in school at Penn State. Like so many other families, it was an IBM job transfer that brought the Harrises to Raleigh.

Kris has entered the craft and culinary competitions ten times since moving south in 1983, winning 24 ribbons in baking alone. It's not the prize money that motivates her. "I like winning the ribbons," she said.

She learned how to make her blue-ribbon-winning German Apple Cake from her grandmother, but the recipe has been around so long no one can remember where it came from. Kris follows her recipes "pretty close to the letter," and doesn't experiment much. Trying to get too elaborate or unusual can hurt your chances of winning.

Kris thinks the judges "like the simple things."

"If you're going to bake a blueberry muffin, they like to taste the blueberries," she says. "You don't need a lot of embellishment."

Some folks rush right over to the fair on opening day to see if they've won. Not Kris. She doesn't want anyone to call up and tell her about it, either.

"I don't want to know until I can see it myself. We wait 'til the kids are out of school and we can take a whole day to go together, as a family."

In spite of her admiration for old-fashioned ways, Kris admits that using a bread machine helps save time. To a mother of three young children, every spare moment is one to cherish.

The Harris kids enjoy spending time in the kitchen, too, getting their hands in the dough and helping Mom cut out cookies. Seven-year-old Daniel has already won his first ribbon for crafts; younger

Like the pioneers she read about as a child, Kris Harris sews, cooks, bakes and quilts.

sisters Kate and Jennifer will likely follow the tradition, as well.

Kris has won ribbons for her biscuits, but hesitates to claim a secret. "They're 'hit-or-miss,'" she says. "The way you handle the dough is important."

She thinks re-rolling the dough too many times may affect rising. "Not being a Southerner, I don't have much experience in biscuits!" Kris says with a laugh.

Kris' latest project flutters in the breeze — it's an appliqued flag she made after discovering how much they cost in stores. She now designs banners for each season and for holidays, and still takes the time to sew Easter and Christmas outfits for the girls.

If there is a secret to Kris Harris' success, it's her outlook. "I just like to do it, and I don't mind spending the time. I don't buy pre-made things because I know I can make them better."

She muses, "Sometimes I wonder if I was born in the wrong era."

Apple Pumpkin Streusel Muffins
by Kris Harris

For streusel topping:
- 2   tablespoons flour
- 1/3 cup sugar
- 1/2 teaspoon cinnamon
- 4   teaspoons butter

For muffins:
- 2 1/2 cups flour
- 2   cups sugar
- 1   tablespoon pumpkin pie spice
- 1   teaspoon baking soda
- 1/2 teaspoon salt
- 2   eggs, slightly beaten
- 1   cup cooked or canned pumpkin
- 1/2 cup vegetable oil
- 2   cups peeled, finely chopped apples

Preheat oven to 350 degrees. Grease a muffin tin and set aside.

First, prepare streusel topping: Mix together flour, sugar and cinnamon, then cut in butter with your fingers or with a pastry blender. Blend just until crumbly. Set aside.

In a large bowl, mix together flour, sugar, pumpkin pie spice, baking soda and salt.

In another bowl, combine eggs, pumpkin and oil. Add to the dry ingredients and stir until just moistened. Stir in apples and spoon into muffin tin, filling each cup only about 3/4 full.

Sprinkle the streusel topping evenly over the muffins. Bake for 25 to 35 minutes, or until an inserted toothpick comes out clean. Remove from pan to cool.

Yield: About 18 muffins

German Apple Cake
by Kris Harris

      5   baking apples
      5   teaspoons sugar
      2   tablespoons cinnamon
      4   eggs
      2   cups sugar
      1   cup oil
      2   teaspoons vanilla
    1/3   cup orange juice
          dash salt
      3   cups flour
      1   teaspoon baking powder
  2 1/2   teaspoons baking soda

Preheat oven to 350 degrees. Grease a bundt pan and set aside.

Peel the apples and cut into small chunks. Mix with the 5 teaspoons of sugar and the cinnamon; set aside.

In a large bowl, mix together the eggs, sugar, oil, vanilla, orange juice and salt. Add flour, baking powder and baking soda. Mix by hand or with mixer (set on low speed) for 1 minute.

Pour 1/3 of the batter into the prepared pan. Cover with 1/2 of the apple mixture. Add another 1/3 of the batter, then the remaining apples. End with the last 1/3 of the batter.

Bake for 1 1/2 hours, or until a tester inserted into the cake comes out clean. Remove from oven and cool on rack before removing from pan.

Yield: 12 to 16 servings

Hint

Do not use Delicious apples for this recipe.

Cinnamon Dip
by Kris Harris

8 oz. cream cheese, softened
   2 tablespoons milk
   2 tablespoons brown sugar
   1 teaspoon vanilla
   1 teaspoon cinnamon
1/4 teaspoon nutmeg

Combine all ingredients and blend until smooth. Serve with cookies or fruit slices. Store in refrigerator.
Yield: 1 cup

The ultimate prize: The blue ribbon, awarded to the very best in each category.

Raleigh

Rose Hampton

Family photos grace the walls of every room in his home, but Danny Hampton has never seen them.

"Danny has been blind since birth," his wife Rose explains. She points to a tiny pair of antique eyeglasses hanging in a frame on the living room wall.

"At first the doctors thought these might help him see a little bit, but they soon realized he couldn't see at all."

Rose and Danny knew each other years ago, but fate took a long time to join their lives together. Each had married another, each had children. Then both were widowed. But their paths came together again, and in 1990 they were married — blending their families with a smoothness like one of Rose's prize-winning candies.

Danny's memories are as clear as any sighted person's. He remembered vividly something wonderful and sweet he'd tasted at school. But he couldn't describe to his new wife what it looked like, or even what color it was. So Rose began experimenting, and the result was her blue-ribbon-winning Peanut Butter Fudge.

But it took her until 1994 to work up enough nerve to submit four items to the State Fair for her first try. Her co-workers at the North Carolina Agency for Public Communications have encouraged Rose, once even congratulating her with a "pounding."

She describes the old tradition: "It's wonderful! When a new preacher or young family would come to town, everyone would bring things. One person would give a pound of butter, another a pound of flour, a pound of sugar, and so on. Then they'd present the 'pounding' to the newcomers in a big bushel basket."

Other traditions mean a lot to Rose, too. Her mother, Pearl Jackson, is gone now, but Rose still keeps close at hand a scrap of paper torn from a notebook. On it, written in scratchy pencil, is Pearl's recipe for chocolate pie, dictated many years ago from mother to daughter.

Rose smiles. "My mom could make biscuits as fast as somebody else could take bread out of a wrapper."

But that was a long time ago, back when a young Rose was just learning and made some biscuits that didn't turn out.

"I pushed them aside, got out the cornmeal, and just made

A collage of her ribbons and recipes hangs proudly in Rose Hampton's kitchen.

cornbread instead," she remembers.

Now Rose not only has a grown daughter of her own, but a daughter-in-law and a step-daughter who are eager to learn about cooking. And they have the best kind of teacher. Mixing together food and family, Rose honors the past as she plans for the future, combining the best of the old ways and the new.

Surely Pearl Jackson would be proud to see her daughter now.

Sweet Potato Biscuits
by Rose Hampton

         2   cups sifted all-purpose flour
       2/3   cup sugar
         2   tablespoons baking powder
     1 1/2   teaspoons salt
       1/2   cup vegetable shortening
         2   cups cooked, mashed sweet potatoes
       1/4   cup milk

Preheat oven to 450 degrees. Grease a baking sheet and set aside.
Sift dry ingredients together. Make a well in the center. Add shortening, potatoes and milk. Mix until a soft dough forms. Add more flour as needed if dough is too sticky.
Roll out dough and cut using a biscuit cutter. Place on baking sheet and bake for 12 to 15 minutes.
Yield: 15 to 18

Hints
These have a lovely orange color and a denser texture than most biscuits.
These do not brown as readily as other biscuits, so watch them as they bake to make sure the edges do not burn.

Mayonnaise Biscuits
by Rose Hampton
and "Papa" Wade D. Hampton, Sr.

         2   cups sifted self-rising flour
         1   tablespoon cooking oil or melted butter
         1   tablespoon mayonnaise
         1   cup milk (use buttermilk if you prefer)
       1/4   cup water

Preheat oven to 400 degrees. Lightly grease a muffin tin and set aside.
Mix all ingredients together with a wooden spoon. Don't overmix.

Batter will be the consistency of muffin or pancake batter.
Spoon into muffin tins, about 2/3 full. Bake for 12 minutes.
Yield: 12

Hints
These look like muffins and taste like biscuits!
Brush with butter and return to oven for a moment if you like a browner top.

Chocolate Pie
by Rose Hampton's mother, Pearl Jackson

   2   cups sugar
   5   heaping tablespoons flour
   5   tablespoons cocoa
   3   cups milk
   6   egg yolks (whites will be used in meringue, below)
   1   teaspoon vanilla
1/2   stick butter
   2   baked pie shells, 9" (deep dish)

Combine sugar, flour and cocoa. Add 1 cup milk gradually, mixing well. Add egg yolks and remaining milk. Stir in vanilla and butter.
Cook in a double boiler on medium heat until thickened, stirring constantly, about 10 minutes.
Pour into baked pie shells. Cover with meringue and brown in oven.
Yield: 2 pies, 8 to 10 servings each

Meringue
by Rose Hampton

   6   egg whites
1/2   teaspoon cream of tartar
1/4-1/2   cup sugar

Beat egg whites until frothy. Add cream of tartar. While beating, add sugar one spoonful at a time. Continue beating until stiff peaks form. Cover filled pie with meringue and place under broiler until brown, about 5 minutes. Watch meringue carefully.

Peanut Butter Fudge
by Rose Hampton

3	cups sugar
1 1/2	sticks butter
2/3	cup evaporated milk
7 oz.	jar marshmallow cream
1 1/4	cups smooth peanut butter
1	tablespoon vanilla
1	cup chopped pecans

Butter a 9x13" pan. Set aside.

Butter the sides of a large saucepan (this prevents sugar crystals from sticking).

In the pan, place sugar, butter and milk. Cover with lid and begin cooking on a very low heat. Stir occasionally, using a clean spoon each time. Replace lid each time you stir the mixture.

Gradually increase temperature to a boil, but keep below medium heat to avoid burning. Stir and replace lid as before. This step should take about 30 minutes.

Once mixture reaches a rolling boil (If you use a candy thermometer, this will be at the "soft ball" stage, 234 degrees), remove lid and stir constantly. Boil exactly 6 minutes.

Remove from heat. Add marshmallow cream, peanut butter, vanilla and nuts and mix well until melted.

Pour into pan and spread to a uniform thickness. Cool and cut into pieces.

Yield: 3 to 4 dozen squares

Hints

Don't use baking spray on the pan. It contains too much water.

Use a fresh spoon each time you stir. This prevents cooled sugar crystals from being introduced back into the mixture.

Chocolate Caramel Peanut Squares
by Rose Hampton

The filling:
- 14 oz. caramel candies, wrappers removed
- 1 small can evaporated milk (5 ounces)
- 1/2 stick butter
- 1 cup semi-sweet chocolate chips
- 2 cups salted, roasted peanuts

Put caramels, milk and butter in a saucepan on low heat. Stir until caramels have melted and no chunks remain. Set aside.

The base and topping:
- 6 squares unsweetened chocolate
- 2 sticks butter
- 2 1/2 cups sugar
- 4 eggs
- 2 teaspoons vanilla
- 1 1/2 cups all-purpose flour

Preheat oven to 350 degrees. Grease and flour a 9x13" pan. Set aside.

Melt butter and chocolate in pan (or microwave) until completely melted. Stir. Remove from heat. Add sugar and stir until well blended. Mix in eggs and vanilla.

Stir in flour and mix well. Pour half the mixture into pan. Bake for 15 minutes. Remove from oven, then pour caramel mixture over baked base. Sprinkle with the chocolate chips and peanuts. Cover with remaining uncooked batter and bake for another 25 to 30 minutes.

Remove from oven. Let cool completely. Cut into squares.

Yield: 2 to 3 dozen, depending on size

Hints
Be sure to cool completely before cutting; otherwise the caramel mixture will be runny.

Don't overcook the caramel mixture; heat just until melted.

Cary

Wendy Hamby

They don't have a history of Carolina connections — it was a job that brought them here from their home in Florida. But that didn't stop Wendy Hamby and her family from jumping into the State Fair with both feet.

"We started doing crafts about 11 years ago, to make gifts for the grandparents," Wendy remembers. "We went to our first fair and decided, 'This seems like something we can all do together.'"

Some of the Hamby family recipes came from a collection Wendy's mother had kept. Like many cooks, Wendy wishes her mom — and her grandmother, too — had written down more of those good recipes to pass along. What were their secrets? A special way of mixing? A certain kind of ingredient?

Wendy still wonders. "I never did learn how to make my mother's 'Kolachy,'" she says, describing a light, apricot-filled cookie from her family's native Bohemia.

She believes it's possible to maximize your chance of creating a prize-winning entry. "Throw out everything before you start baking for the fair, and use the freshest ingredients you can find," she advises.

These days, even the family dog, Grizz, enjoys the excitement of getting ready for the fair. "He eats whatever hits the floor," Wendy says with a laugh.

The Hambys have also discovered another avenue of culinary competition: baking with honey. They've mastered the trick of converting recipes that call for sugar and have the ribbons to prove their success. "Things baked with honey are more moist," Wendy claims.

While some bakers are possessive of their secrets, the Hambys are happy to share their hints and recipes. "It's okay with me if someone wants to use my recipe," says Wendy. "If they enter it and win, that means it's a good one."

Wendy Hamby is almost as proud of her blue ribbons as she is of her prize-winning son, Ben.

Yum Yum Squares
by Wendy Hamby

2/3	cup margarine, melted and cooled
1	pound light brown sugar
3	eggs
1	teaspoon vanilla
1	teaspoon water
2 1/2	cups flour
2 1/2	teaspoons baking powder
1	teaspoon salt
6 oz.	chocolate chips
1	cup chopped nuts

Preheat oven to 350 degrees. Grease and flour a 9x13" pan. Set aside.

Beat margarine, sugar, eggs, vanilla and water until blended. Add sifted dry ingredients and mix thoroughly. Add chocolate chips and nuts, blending by hand. Spread into pan and bake for 25 minutes. Cool and cut into squares.

Yield: About 2 dozen.

Carrot Cake
by Wendy Hamby

2	cups flour
2	teaspoons baking soda
2	teaspoons cinnamon
1/2	teaspoon salt
3	eggs
3/4	cup oil
3/4	cup buttermilk
1 1/2	cups sugar
1/4	cup honey
2	teaspoons vanilla
8 oz.	can crushed pineapple, drained
2	cups finely grated carrots
3 1/2	ounces shredded coconut
1	cup chopped nuts

Preheat oven to 350 degrees. Grease and flour 2 9" cake pans and set aside.

Sift flour, soda, cinnamon and salt together. Set aside.

In a large bowl, beat the eggs; add oil, buttermilk, sugar, honey and vanilla, mixing well. Add flour mixture and mix until blended. Add pineapple, carrots, coconut and nuts. Stir well. Pour into prepared pans and bake for 30 minutes, or until a tester inserted into the center comes out clean.

Cool on rack for at least 10 minutes before removing from pans; frost with Cream Cheese Frosting.

Yield: 12 to 14 servings

Hints for working with honey

Honey has greater sweetening power. Substitute 3/4 cup of honey for 1 cup of sugar. Reduce total liquid by 1/4 cup. Add a pinch of baking soda to recipe to prevent it from turning brown. (NOTE: Omit the baking soda if the recipe calls for sour cream.)

Cream Cheese Frosting
by Wendy Hamby

     1/2 cup butter, room temperature
    8 oz. cream cheese, room temperature
      1   teaspoon vanilla
      2   cups confectioners sugar
      1   teaspoon orange juice
      1   teaspoon grated orange peel

Cream butter and cream cheese together until fluffy. Add vanilla, confectioners sugar, orange juice and orange peel. Mix until smooth.
Yield: About 2 1/2 cups

Cranberry Fluffs
by Wendy Hamby

     1/4 cup butter or margarine, room temperature
     3/4 cup brown sugar
      1   egg
      1   teaspoon vanilla
      1   tablespoon grated orange peel
          pinch of salt
     1/4 cup honey
    1 1/2 cups flour
     1/2 teaspoon baking soda
     1/2 cup nuts, chopped
     3/4 cup canned whole cranberry sauce

Preheat oven to 375 degrees. Grease a baking sheet and set aside. Cream together the butter, brown sugar, egg, vanilla, orange peel and salt until light. Add honey and beat well.

In a separate bowl, sift together flour and baking soda. Add to the creamed mixture and stir until well-blended. Stir in nuts, then fold in cranberries.

Drop batter by rounded teaspoonfuls onto prepared baking sheet. Bake for 10 to 12 minutes. Cool on wire rack.

Yield: 3 dozen

Cary

Ben Hamby

Can you: Tell a tangent from a triangle? Convert kilometers to miles? And bake a prize-winning chocolate cake?

Answer "yes" to all of the above, if you're Ben Hamby.

It would be enough if all he did was excel in baking — but Ben's bookshelves are crammed full of trophies for sports and commendations for academics, too. The high school sophomore competes regularly — with not only the smartest students but the best bakers in the state. And he wins more often than he loses.

While older brother Mike concentrated on schoolwork, Ben took time out — his favorite basketball team, Florida, had already been eliminated from the NCAA basketball playoffs — to talk about his own winning streak.

The list is a long one: cakes, cookies, fudge, brownies, muffins, candy and crafts. The Hamby family has more than a hundred ribbons to prove their expertise in all those categories.

From the time they were little, both Mike and Ben got involved in family crafts projects, making gifts for their grandparents. From there, it was a natural progression to wall hangings, Christmas ornaments and chocolate-covered Easter eggs.

Ben has won ribbons every year, even the ever-elusive ribbon for true pound cake, although he no longer enters that category. That's because, "It seems like 900 people enter pound cakes."

He pulls a giant silver-blue ribbon from the bundle of smaller ones. Asked about its meaning, he's modest as he explains, "This one's a 'sweepstakes ribbon.' It's awarded to the person who wins the most individual ribbons." If you enter and win enough categories, the extra money from the prize awards can really add up — a nice bonus for a student.

Ben isn't really a purist for technique; he's one of only a handful of winners who admit using products like "Pam." He doesn't bother with buttering and flouring his baking pans, saying, "Just spray 'em!"

Maybe competition just comes naturally to the Hamby family. For them, entering the State Fair is part of their new family tradition. They've discovered that teamwork is essential, whether the contest is in candy or calculus, and whether it takes place in the Quiz Bowl or the

Not just a winner in the kitchen, Ben Hamby's shelves are full of awards for his academic and athletic achievements, too.

kitchen.

Ben shares one last insight. "Cook for the fun of it. Enjoy it — Don't worry about the competition."

Easter Eggs
by Ben Hamby

  1/2 stick margarine, room temperature
    2 ounces cream cheese
    1 pound confectioners' sugar
  12 ounces creamy peanut butter
    2 14-ounce bags of candy melts

Mix margarine and cream cheese until smooth. Slowly add sugar until well blended. Add peanut butter, mixing well. Mixture will be crumbly. Shape into bite-sized eggs and place on a wax-paper-lined cookie sheet.

Melt half the candy melts at a time in microwave or in double boiler on stove, being careful to follow package directions for temperature and length of time to heat. Dip eggs into melted chocolate and, using a fork or toothpick, place the dipped eggs on another wax-paper-lined sheet.

Allow to cool. Wrap in aluminum foil, or store-bought candy wrapping. Keep refrigerated.

Yield: About 60 small Easter eggs

Hints

You can buy candy melts and specially-designed candy "dipper" spoons at candy-making supply and craft stores.

Don't overheat the chocolate; if it gets too hot it will lose its sheen and become too thick. If this occurs, stir in a tablespoon of solid vegetable shortening.

Once you've finished dipping the eggs, you can dip fruits, nuts or cookies in the leftover chocolate. Try sugar or peanut butter cookies.

French Chocolate Cake
by Ben Hamby

```
1/2    cup butter
1 1/2  cups sugar
1/2    cup milk
1 3/4  cups cake flour
1      teaspoon cream of tartar
2      eggs, beaten
2      packets, 1 ounce each, Nestle unsweetened Choco-Bake OR
2      squares baking chocolate, melted
1      teaspoon baking soda, dissolved in 3/4 cup boiling water
```

Preheat oven to 350 degrees. Grease and lightly flour 2 9" cake pans. Set aside.

Cream butter well. Add sugar gradually, then add 1 tablespoon of the measured milk. Beat until fluffy.

Sift flour and measure. Add cream of tartar and sift again.

Begin adding flour to the creamed ingredients a little at a time, alternately with the milk. Once you have added about 1/3 of the flour and milk, add the beaten eggs. Then add the rest of the flour and milk alternately.

Blend in melted chocolate. Add hot water and baking soda mixture last, stirring it in gently.

Pour batter into prepared pans and bake 30 to 35 minutes, or until a tester inserted into the center comes out clean. Remove from oven and allow to cool for at least 10 minutes before removing cakes from pans. Frost with Buttercream Frosting.

Yield: 8 to 10 servings

Buttercream Frosting
by Ben Hamby

1/2 cup solid vegetable shortening
1/2 cup butter
  2 cups sifted confectioners sugar
  1 egg white, unbeaten
  1 tablespoon cream or milk
1/2 teaspoon vanilla
  2 squares of baking chocolate, melted

Cream butter and shortening well. Gradually add 1 cup of the sugar. Add the egg white, then the remaining sugar, cream or milk and vanilla. Add the chocolate last.

Yield: About 3 cups

Hints
If you don't wish to use recipes that contain raw eggs, you may substitute any other frosting recipe.

Wait till cake has fully cooled to frost.

Raleigh

Cheryl Hall

It can be frustrating. You know your recipe is a good one. It's won first prize before. So what happened this year?

Cheryl Hall knows that feeling. She's entered cheese straws every year since 1979 and won 11 ribbons — but she can't explain about the years she didn't win. Perhaps it's the judges' changing likes and dislikes.

"One year, the judge wrote on my entry 'Too light in color,'" Cheryl recalled. "But the next year a WHITE cheddar cheese straw took the blue ribbon."

For 15 years, Cheryl worked in a large office full of co-workers "willing to have a party for any excuse."

"Birthdays, baby showers — even St. Patrick's Day," she said.

That was how she started baking regularly, making snacks for those parties and getting much praise for them.

But even she still suffers an occasional disaster.

"I will admit to a big flop about two weeks ago," Cheryl says. "I was making a coffee cake for breakfast and I followed the directions from my *Betty Crocker Cookbook*. It overflowed, even though I used the size pan the recipe called for."

Still, she considers that cookbook a good one. That's where she learned about baking bread and pies. Today, her favorite recipes are some she "cobbled together." One — a muffin recipe containing bran, nuts, bananas and honey — has won the State Fair's honey competition.

She doesn't care for bread machines.

"I like to put my hands in the dough," she says.

She picks up a plastic-bagged loaf from the grocery store and shakes her head. "But *this* is what my husband Charles likes."

Of the two kinds of cookware in Cheryl's kitchen — cast iron and Calphalon — she prefers the old-fashioned iron. The only gadget she really uses is her cookie press; it's perfect for making her famous cheese straws.

Cheryl has learned to pay close attention to the rules when entering the State Fair. Sometimes they change, ever so slightly.

"For a long time, the fair required six muffins in your entry. Now

No one comes close to Cheryl Hall's success, year after year, for melt-in-your-mouth cheese wafers and straws.

it's four. In cheese straws, it was a dozen; now it's six."

She also knows that people entering the fair take the competition very seriously. Cheryl heard of a woman so anxious to learn if she'd won that she sneaked into the fair the night before it opened, posted a friend as a sentry at the door, and stole a look to see whose plate held the blue ribbon.

Sometimes it's hard to explain why people compete, Cheryl thinks, but victories, however small, are satisfying.

"Even if it's just a pat on the back," she says, "that's one of life's rewards."

Cheese Straws or Wafers
by Cheryl Hall

     2   sticks unsalted butter, softened
  8 oz. sharp cheddar cheese, grated
     2   cups all-purpose flour
   1/2   teaspoon salt, or to taste
   1/4   teaspoon red pepper, or to taste

Preheat oven to 400 degrees.

In a large mixing bowl, cream butter and cheese together. Mix in salt and pepper, blending well. Stir in flour; dough will be stiff.

To make straws: Fill barrel of cookie press with dough and press out onto ungreased cookie sheet. Bake about 8 minutes. Remove from oven and let cool slightly before slicing into strips of desired length.

To make wafers: Form dough into rolls of desired diameter. Wrap in plastic and refrigerate. Chill until firm, about 2 to 3 hours. Cut into wafers about 1/4" thick. Bake on ungreased cookie sheet for about 10 minutes.

Yield: 4 dozen

Bourbon Pecan Pie
by Cheryl Hall

   1/2   stick unsalted butter, melted
     1   cup white sugar
     1   cup dark corn syrup
     3   eggs
   1/4   teaspoon salt
   2-3   tablespoons bourbon OR 1 teaspoon vanilla
     1   cup pecans, coarsely chopped, plus whole pecans for garnish
     1   9" unbaked pie shell

Preheat oven to 350 degrees.

Blend together the butter, sugar, corn syrup and eggs. Mix in salt, bourbon and pecans until well-blended.

Pour into pie shell. Place whole pecans on top of filling. Bake 45 to 55 minutes. Let cool completely before slicing.

Yield: 8 to 10 servings

"Bran-Nana" Honey Muffins
by Cheryl Hall

```
1 1/2   cups bran cereal
  3/4   cup milk
    1   egg
    1   cup ripe bananas, mashed (about 3)
  1/3   cup vegetable oil
  1/4   cup honey
1 1/4   cups all-purpose flour
    3   teaspoons baking powder
  1/2   teaspoon salt
  1/4   teaspoon cinnamon
  1/2   cup chopped walnuts or pecans, optional
```

Preheat oven to 425 degrees. Grease a muffin tin or place paper liners in each cup. Set aside.

Combine cereal and milk in a large mixing bowl. Set aside for 10 minutes to allow cereal to soften. Blend in egg, bananas, oil and honey.

In a separate bowl, combine flour, baking powder, salt, cinnamon and nuts. Add to cereal mixture and stir only until combined.

Pour into muffin cups. Bake 20 to 25 minutes. Remove from pan while hot and allow to cool on wire rack.

Yield: 1 dozen

Hint

Very high in fiber.

Durham

Edna Foust

She'd heard the story her whole life, and no one could say it wasn't true. Her grandfather, Lafayette Coble, was the first black man to own land in Alamance County. As a boy he'd been a slave, carrying water for the Confederate troops during the war. When the Union Army came through, Lafayette's mother hid him in a nearby thicket until the soldiers passed. It was a few years later, after the war was over, that a man named Mr. Cooper sold an 88-acre piece of land to Lafayette.

It was on that land that Edna Foust grew up.

Her story is a different one. Edna never married or had children. An adopted brother was killed many years ago. So it might have seemed natural for Edna to continue working the family farm. But she thought there was more to life than that. She "got the wish" when she was little to become a nurse, and she made that wish come true. She went to school in Richmond, but returned home to North Carolina to practice.

With no one to keep the family farm going, the land was sold many years ago, but Edna's decision served her well regardless.

Her career took her through 46 years at a half-dozen hospitals, and after that, she was ready to retire — or so she thought.

"I was miserable!" she exclaims, "I couldn't sit still."

So in spite of recent foot surgery, she's back at work, part-time at the Durham County Hospital. She enjoys the patients and staff too much to stay away.

Her work, however, doesn't keep her from from baking, something it took her a while to learn.

As a young girl, she tried to make a cake by imitating her mother.

"It fell," she says. "I carried it to the pig pen and fed it to the hogs."

Laughing, Edna has to stop and catch her breath before she continues, "Then I cleaned up, washed up everything before my parents came in from the fields."

It was a long time before she tried again.

Over the years, however, she got a lot of practice. Birthdays, anniversaries, weddings sparked her to fire her oven. But she didn't need a special occasion to bake for others. She remembered a cake she baked for her dentist. She took it on a Wednesday afternoon, and first

New to competition, Edna Foust won a blue ribbon the first time she entered the State Fair.

thing Thursday morning the phone rang.

"Edna — the cake is gone already!" the dentist groaned.

She hasn't any secrets, just an old-fashioned attitude about what works; lots of careful mixing and simple ingredients. So it was only right that Edna would win a blue ribbon — and she did, the first time she entered the State Fair in 1992.

Her home of 20 years is full of special touches. The drapes and sofa match the silk flowers she has specially arranged. She's got her Kitchen-aid mixer, her big-screen TV and a nice, comfortable chair, but she'll never forget an earlier time.

The little girl who picked cotton and attended a one-room schoolhouse has seen a lot of things change, but she knows what ought to stay the same.

"Wash clean, don't make a mess, follow the rules, sweep under the bed — and in the corners."

And she offers one more piece of advice that she's always carried with her, one that has served her especially well in her baking: "Whatever you do, do it well."

Edna's Old Fashioned Pound Cake by Edna Foust

```
  1  cup butter
  1  cup vegetable shortening
  3  cups sugar
  6  eggs
  4  cups cake flour
1/4  teaspoon salt
  1  teaspoon baking powder
  1  cup milk
  1  teaspoon almond flavoring or vanilla
```

Preheat oven to 300 degrees. Grease and flour a 10" tube pan. Set aside.

In a large bowl, cream butter and shortening until well-blended. Add sugar gradually until fluffy. Add eggs, one at a time, beating well after each addition.

In a separate bowl, sift then measure flour. Add salt and baking powder.

Combine milk and flavoring in a measuring cup. With mixer on low speed, add the flour mixture, alternately with the milk, to the butter mixture. Begin and end with flour. Pour batter into pan. Bake 1 1/2 hours or until a tester inserted in cake comes out clean. Remove from oven and cool in pan on wire rack before inverting on plate to serve.

Yield: 12 to 16 servings

Hint
Edna likes to use the old-fashioned aluminum baking pans, "because that's the kind my mama used."

Apex

Marie Jones and Linda Carpenter

White Oak, Olive Chapel and Green Level — even the names of these little communities bring to mind another time. A time when neighbors were like family, and family was the most important part of life.

Linda Carpenter and Marie Jones are lucky. Neighbors for ten years, they live a kind of life that may be disappearing. With a closeness shared only by the best of friends, they laugh easily, sometimes finishing each other's sentences.

Marie remembers, "When we moved out here, over 20 years ago, there were only three families on this road." Even though Marie was born in California, Linda is quick to point out that her friend might as well be a native, "Because she was raised here in North Carolina."

Marie was the first of the two to begin entering the State Fair. What got Linda started?

"Her!" Linda says, nodding to her friend across the kitchen table.

Both are now fair winners, and as they sip iced tea on a sunny spring afternoon, Linda recalls her early experiences in competition.

"At first I was overwhelmed, but Marie is good at egging people on."

They always go to the fair together on opening day to see who's won.

"We have a ham biscuit and a cup of coffee," Marie says. "Then we go check our ribbons."

And what happens if one wins and the other doesn't?

"We congratulate each other and take pictures," says Marie.

Marie and Linda share many interests. Both are mothers. Both love horses, cooking, canning and crafts. Both came from families where baking was a regular part of life, and neither cares much for fancy equipment, for food processors and such. Does either have a bread machine?

"No!" they answer, emphatically and in unison.

But there are differences, too, in style and approach.

Marie: "I try to put something in the fair every year."

Marie Jones, left, and Linda Carpenter are good neighbors, friendly competitors and State Fair blue-ribbon winners.

Linda: "When it gets close to the time to enter, I say, 'I can't do it. I don't have anything to enter.' But the next thing you know, here I am, up till two in the morning trying to get those cookies baked...."

Marie: "We think about it all year."

Linda: "But we really get started in September."

Marie's ribbons are on display in her home. Where are Linda's? "In the attic!" she admits.

Since contestants aren't allowed to see the judging take place, it can be hard to understand why one entry wins and another doesn't. Beyond the obvious mistakes, Linda and Marie feel it's partly a matter of each judge's personal taste that decides the outcome. They've seen a former blue ribbon entry not win so much as an honorable mention in subsequent years.

And both know that even expert bakers have disasters sometimes.

"All that work and you might not have something to carry to the fair," Linda says, shaking her head.

Stepping outside into the afternoon sun, Linda and Marie call their horses back to the barn to be photographed. Mih Dream, Linda's Arabian gelding, is skittish when faced with the camera. Ben, Marie's quarterhorse, ignores the commotion, aloof from his side of the fence. In the distance, traffic hums.

The state is widening the highway that runs past the Carpenter and Jones family land, a harbinger of changing times.

These two friends realize that the nature of small towns and rural areas is changing, but both find comfort in traditional things—their gardens, pastures, kitchens, and especially in their families and friendship.

Double Chocolate Peanut Butter Thumbprint Cookies by Linda Carpenter

```
1 1/2  cups all-purpose flour
  1/2  cup cocoa
1 1/2  teaspoons baking powder
  1/4  teaspoon salt
    2  cups chocolate chips
    1  cup sugar
    1  cup peanut butter (do not use "all-natural" peanut butter)
  1/3  cup butter or margarine, softened
1 1/2  teaspoons vanilla
    2  eggs
```

Two hours before baking:
Combine flour, cocoa, baking powder and salt in a bowl and set aside.

Over low heat, melt 1 cup of chocolate chips in a saucepan and stir until smooth. Remove from heat.

In a bowl, cream together the sugar, 1/3 cup of peanut butter, butter and vanilla. Beat in the melted chocolate. Add eggs, one at a time, beating well after each addition. Gradually beat in blended dry ingredients. Stir in remaining chocolate chips. Cover and chill dough until firm, about 2 hours.

To bake cookies:
Preheat oven to 350 degrees.

Shape dough into balls about 1 1/2" in diameter. Place on an ungreased baking sheet about 2" apart. Press thumb into the top of each cookie. Fill each depression with about 1/2 teaspoon of the remaining peanut butter. Bake 10 to 15 minutes. Remove from oven and let cool on wire rack.

Yield: About 3 dozen

Chocolate Kiss Macaroons
by Marie Jones

1/3	cup butter or margarine, softened
3	ounces cream cheese, softened
3/4	cup sugar
1	egg yolk
2	teaspoons almond extract
2	teaspoons orange juice
1 1/4	cups all-purpose flour
2	teaspoons baking powder
1/4	teaspoon salt
14 oz.	flaked coconut
9 oz.	chocolate kiss candies, wrappers removed

One hour before baking:
Preheat oven to 350 degrees.

In a large mixing bowl, cream together butter, cream cheese and sugar until fluffy. Add egg yolk, almond extract and orange juice and beat well. In another bowl, combine the flour, baking powder and salt, add gradually to the creamed mixture. Stir in all but 3/4 cup of the coconut. Set remainder aside. Cover and chill dough 1 hour, or until it can be handled easily.

To bake cookies:
Shape dough into balls 1" in diameter, then roll in remaining coconut. Place on an ungreased cookie sheet. Bake 10 to 12 minutes, or until lightly browned. Remove from oven; before cookies begin to cool, press an unwrapped chocolate kiss on the top of each. Cool 1 minute, then remove to a wire rack to finish cooling.

Yield: 4 to 5 dozen cookies

Hints
Watch to make sure coconut doesn't burn.

Cary

Lil Seastrom

It was 1952 and George Seastrom was boasting about his wife's "Hawaiian Pie." From Hampton, Virginia, he submitted Lil's recipe to a nationwide baking contest he heard about on the radio.

Before she even knew what had happened, Lil Seastrom's lemon-pineapple-coconut creation had won. Somebody called her from New York to tell her about the fabulous prizes she would receive.

"A toaster and a steam iron!" she recalls, chuckling.

An aunt provided Lil's earliest inspiration to bake. "I loved to go to her house — everything tasted so good. I wanted my baking to be like hers."

George worked for the Public Health Service, and the Seastrom family moved first to Pennsylvania, then to Maryland, later to Virginia and California.

"Then back to North Carolina," Lil recalls, "then California again — back and forth three times — and Washington and Illinois...."

But it was in New Mexico that friends first encouraged Lil to begin competing at state fairs, in the gardening categories. Out West, the combination of climate and varying elevations create stunning differences in the flowers that grow there. "The sun and the soil make the colors seem more vibrant," Lil explains. "Back then, I was too involved with flowers to care much about what was going on with the baking categories."

The same high altitudes that affect vegetation also pose problems for baking. Lil remembers, "In Albuquerque, the gas company held cooking schools to teach us how to use our appliances."

Over the years, Lil has learned what ensures success in the kitchen. "I follow recipes. I'd have the biggest mess you ever saw if I didn't. All you have to do is forget one ingredient and the recipe won't turn out like it's supposed to."

It may seem surprising, but the Seastroms have kept in touch with the friends they made while moving from place to place. "When you're 'transient' like we were, you make friends easily," Lil says. "Some of those friendships are very lasting."

Just recently, 20 of those friends, going back more than 20 years, reunited.

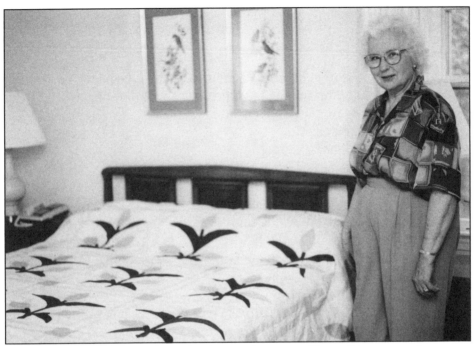

Whether creating a prize-winning cake or quilt, patience and perseverance make the difference, as Lil Seastrom knows.

Lil enjoys trying new recipes for her guests.

"I've got an 'experimental' kitchen," she says with a laugh. "When I have company for dinner, they never know what they're going to get!"

For holidays, Lil's prize-winning baked goods become some of her friends' most anticipated gifts. Months in advance, she's already prepared and frozen the candied grapefruit shells to be filled with fruitcake next Christmas.

Her philosophy about competing is simple. Lil says, "It's a challenge. It takes a lot of work, and most people just don't want to put forth that effort."

But anybody willing to make the effort, follow the recipe and keep trying for that ribbon can eventually win one, Lil believes.

"If you want something bad enough you can get it."

"Pretty Goody"
by Lil Seastrom

     1   cup pecans or almonds, ground to a paste in blender
     3   sticks butter or margarine, softened
     1   cup sugar
     4   eggs, separated
   1/2   teaspoon almond extract
   1/2   teaspoon vanilla
     2   cups sifted flour
   1/4   teaspoon salt
   1/8   teaspoon green food coloring
   1/8   teaspoon red food coloring
 12 oz. peach or apricot preserves
     4   squares semi-sweet chocolate

Preheat oven to 350 degrees. Grease 3 9x13" pans, line with wax paper and grease again. Set aside.

In a large bowl, combine the ground nuts, butter, sugar, egg yolks, almond extract and vanilla. Beat until light and fluffy. Stir in flour and salt.

In a separate bowl, beat egg whites until stiff peaks form. Fold gently into batter.

Pour 1/3 of batter into first pan. Spread evenly. Divide the remaining batter into 2 bowls, add the green food coloring to one and add the red food coloring to the other. Pour each colored batter into the remaining 2 pans.

Bake for 15 minutes or until edges are golden brown. Layers will be thin. Remove from oven, turn out of pans and cool on wire racks.

When cakes are cooled and you are ready to assemble, heat preserves. Place the green layer on a cookie sheet. Spread half the preserves over cake. Slide the yellow layer on top; spread with remaining preserves. Top with red layer. Cover with plastic wrap and refrigerate at least 1 hour.

Melt chocolate in a double boiler. Spread carefully only on top of assembled cake. Let dry 30 minutes before slicing. Trim off any rough edges or places where chocolate may have dripped.

Cut into small squares, about 1"

Yield: 5 to 6 dozen

Hints

The food coloring is optional.
Lil says these freeze well and are great for holidays.
This recipe has been in her family for many years.

Coconut Layer Cake
by Lil Seastrom

The cake:

      1   cup butter (or 1/2 butter and 1/2 margarine)
      2   cups sugar
      4   eggs
      3   cups cake flour
      1   scant tablespoon baking powder
    1/2   teaspoon salt
    1/2   cup buttermilk
    1/2   cup water
      1   teaspoon vanilla

Preheat oven to 375 degrees. Grease and flour 3 - 9" cake pans and set aside.

In a large bowl, cream butter till light. Add sugar. Blend in eggs, one at a time, beating well after each addition.

In a separate bowl, sift together the flour, baking powder and salt.

Mix together the water and buttermilk. Add to the creamed mixture alternately with the flour, blending well. Stir in vanilla.

Pour into prepared pans and bake about 20 minutes, or until a tester inserted into the center of cake comes out clean. Do not overbake. Remove from oven and allow to cool 5 minutes before turning out onto wire rack.

The filling:

           Milk of 1 large coconut + whole milk to equal 1 cup OR
      1   cup unsweetened coconut milk
           Meat of 1 large coconut, grated OR
      1   package frozen coconut, thawed
      2   cups sugar
      2   tablespoons cornstarch

Set aside 3/4 cup of grated coconut. In a saucepan, mix remaining coconut with milk, sugar and cornstarch. Cook over medium heat and stir until thickened. Allow to cool slightly.

Between each layer, spread filling, then sprinkle with reserved grated coconut. Make sure to leave enough for top and sides of cake.

Spread filling on top and sides of cake. Sprinkle with remaining coconut.

Yield: 12 to 16 servings

Candied Grapefruit Shells
by Lil Seastrom

4   large grapefruits
sugar and water in equal amounts, enough to cover fruit
salt

The day before baking the fruitcakes:
Halve each grapefruit, using a zig-zag cutting pattern. Remove fruit sections from the shells and save for another use. Scrape the white membrane from the inside of the shells, using care not to cut through the peel.

Place in a large pan and cover with water to which has been added 2 teaspoons of salt. Bring to a boil and cook 10 minutes. Drain water. Repeat 3 times to remove bitterness from the peel. Drain and allow to cool.

Using the same pan, combine equal amounts of water and sugar (enough to cover the fruit in the next step). Cook to a medium thick syrup. Remove from heat.

Place fruit in syrup and let stand for 24 hours, turning several times.
The next day:
Place the pan on medium heat and cook to a very thick syrup. Remove from heat and carefully place each candied shell, inverted, on a wire rack to cool. Or, each shell may be placed over a small bowl.

When cool, fill with fruitcake mixture and bake according to cake recipe.

Yield: 8 shells for filling

Hints
Use thin-skinned fruit.
These may be frozen for filling later.

Fruitcake
by Lil Seastrom
To be baked in candied grapefruit shells or 2 loaf pans

1	package yellow cake mix
1/2	cup applesauce
4	eggs
1	teaspoon salt
1	teaspoon orange extract
2	cups chopped dates
8 oz.	candied pineapple, cut into strips
8 oz.	candied red cherries
4	cups nuts, broken
1/2	cup flour

Preheat oven to 275 degrees. Grease a large cookie sheet (or 2 loaf pans if not using candied shells) and set aside.

Into a mixing bowl, place the cake mix, applesauce, eggs, salt and orange extract. Beat until smooth, about 3 minutes. Then add the dates, pineapple, cherries, nuts and flour. Blend well.

Fill each shell nearly full with batter. Bake for 2 1/4 hours. Cool, then wrap in cellophane and refrigerate 2 to 4 weeks before serving.

To serve, slice each candied shell in sections.

Yield: 8 filled candied shells or 2 loaves

Hint
If using loaf pans, bake for 2 1/2 hours. Follow directions for storing.

Baker's Hint
by Lil Seastrom

Equal amounts of:
> Flour
> Oil
> Shortening

Mix together and store in refrigerator. Use to grease baking pans.

Hint
Lil says this keeps a long time and works in any kind of baking pan.

Cary

Holly Caskey

Life can turn shaky without warning. Holly Caskey remembers the day, back in 1989, when the earthquake hit near her home in Northern California. Her husband had just driven over three Bay Area bridges during his two-hour daily commute.

"Brian had been home about 15 minutes when that bridge collapsed," Holly recalls. "That was when we made our final decision. We said, 'OK, we're going to move to North Carolina.'"

She can't even count the number of earthquakes she's lived through. "It was just a part of growing up in California," Holly says with a shrug.

It always takes time for a new place to feel like home. Sometimes, it's the little things that don't quite fit. Holly smiles, thinking how surprised she was the first time people driving by — people she didn't even know — would wave at her from their cars. But in a few short years, the Caskeys have gotten to know almost all their neighbors.

The Solono County Fair, back in California, was where Holly first competed and won a ribbon with her mother's recipe for English Toffee. She considers her blue ribbon — for her first entry at the North Carolina State Fair — "a fluke," but admits she's intrigued enough to enter again.

One of Holly's most-requested recipes is "edible, but not tasty" — her version of play clay. Daughters Tabitha and McKenzie enjoy making the "globby" stuff at a fraction of the cost of store-bought clays. For more palatable dishes, Holly still uses the *Better Homes and Gardens Cookbook*, which Brian gave her their first Christmas together.

Most cooks are particular about their pans, and Holly is no exception. She reaches into her kitchen cabinet and pulls out two loaf pans. Both are battered and discolored, but she prizes them for more than their ability to bake perfect bread.

"My grandfather came to America from Scotland in the 1920s," she says. "He later opened a bakery in Southern California."

When the bakery closed, Holly's parents inherited the bread pans.

"My mom gave them to me," Holly says.

The Caskeys are becoming part of a new breed of North Carolinians. They like the slower pace of life in the state, and they

Holly Caskey still uses these bread pans from her grandfather's bakery in California.

don't miss the earthquakes a bit. "I couldn't move back now," Holly says.

Now it's Holly who finds herself explaining local customs to her relatives. "When my dad visited us, he saw people drive by and wave. He'd ask, 'Who's that?'

"I'd answer, 'I don't know.'

"And he'd ask, 'Then why are you waving?'"

So if you find yourself driving through Holly's neighborhood, slow down when you pass by her house. It's the one with the rose bushes right in the front. And if you feel like waving, go right ahead — everyone living there knows to wave back.

English Toffee
by Holly Caskey's mother, Margie Gray

          1   pound butter, salted
          2   cups sugar
          1   cup water
          1   cup almonds, chopped
        1/2   pound chocolate, either milk or semi-sweet, shredded or chips
        1/2   cup ground walnuts or pecans

With butter, grease a cookie sheet (one with sides) or jelly roll pan and set aside.

In a 4-quart saucepan, bring butter, sugar and water to a boil. Add almonds and stir until temperature reaches 300 degrees on a candy thermometer. This step can take up to 1 hour. Once mixture reaches 300 degrees, remove from heat and immediately spread into prepared pan. Sprinkle with chocolate, then walnuts.

Refrigerate until cool. Turn out onto a clean towel and crack candy into pieces of desired size. Store, refrigerated, in a tin.

Yield: About 2 pounds

Hints

Do not use baking sprays to grease pans; the water they contain will leave bubbles or cracks.

Candy temperatures rise at varying speeds, so watch carefully.

Work quickly when spreading into pan — candy sets up fast!

Holly's mother makes her toffee with the nuts and chocolate on the bottom. If you want to try it her way, just put the walnuts in the pan first, followed by the chocolate. Then spread the cooked candy mixture on top.

Play Clay for Kids
by Holly Caskey

  1   cup flour
1/4   cup salt
  2   tablespoons cream of tartar
  1   cup water
  2   teaspoons food coloring
  1   tablespoon vegetable oil
      Flour for kneading

Mix together the flour, salt and cream of tartar. In another bowl, combine the water, food coloring and oil.

In a saucepan, place the flour mixture, then add the liquid. Cook over medium heat about 3 to 5 minutes, but do not allow mixture to reach a boil. Mixture will not be smooth, but when it begins to form a ball, turn out onto a floured surface. Knead until the stickiness is gone.

Store in airtight plastic container or zipper bag.

Yield: About 2 cups

Hints

If your kids tend to put everything they find into their mouths, this clay is a non-toxic alternative to store-bought clays. It also washes easily out of clothing.

Older kids can use their imaginations, adding glitter to the clay and creating their own colors.

Durham

Joanna Wolfe

Asked her opinion about bread-making machines, Joanna Wolfe shows off one that's been in her family a while.

The pitted metal bucket resembles the modern bread machine about as much as a covered wagon looks like a Ferrari. She reads the directions, stamped into the lid: "Place ingredients inside and turn crank...."

Laughter erupts in Joanna's kitchen.

Though it was a job transfer that brought her to the South, Joanna says she's "extremely happy" in North Carolina. As a self-described "P.K." (Preacher's Kid), she lived in a lot of different places. But North Carolina's home now.

A computer network manager, Joanna has access to the best of modern technology. In her kitchen, though, it's a different story. She still does things the old-fashioned way.

The secret to her prize-winning Angel Food Cake isn't a fancy appliance or some exotic flavoring. It's a flat, metal whisk, designed to whip air up into the batter. "Mixers stir ingredients down," Joanna explains.

Today, she's making brownies. "I make them about 40 times a year," she says, and dictates the recipe off the top of her head.

"It's important to keep the ingredients in the right order," she adds.

Then she elaborates, "If you mix the sugar and cocoa first, then add the butter, the brownies will be 'caky.'

"But if you mix the sugar and butter first, then add the cocoa, they'll be more 'fudgy.'"

A small distinction? Maybe, maybe not.

When State Fair judges are faced with dozens of entries in a single category, even a tiny variation can make the difference between winning and losing. "A choc-o-holic's dream," one of the judges wrote on Joanna's entry tag.

The only time she can recall something not turning out was an experiment she tried. Joanna substituted shortening for the margarine in her Brownie recipe, baked up a batch, and took the treats to work. No one commented, but it was the only time she can remember any brownies left at the end of the day.

Joanna Wolfe smiles as she holds a "bread machine" designed to save time in the kitchens of generations past.

"They just didn't taste right," she recalls. "I'll never do that again."

Joanna didn't let that little mishap dampen her enthusiasm. Her recipes are so consistently foolproof that she has tackled the one confection that strikes fear in the hearts of even experienced bakers — the wedding cake.

Joanna's made several. The most recent took four days and she remembers every detail: "Carrot Cake with Pecan Fondant filling — and cream cheese icing." Would she do it again?

That depends. The amount of work, time and attention needed to create a culinary masterpiece is considerable. To really do it right, you can't cut corners or save any steps.

So for now, Joanna is sticking with her tried-and-true winners: Brownies, Angel Food Cake and Shortbread.

She's adamant. "The next wedding cake I bake is going to be my own!"

Brownies
by Joanna Wolfe

2	sticks margarine
2	cups sugar
1	cup powdered cocoa, unsweetened
1	teaspoon vanilla
1	teaspoon salt
4	eggs
1 1/4	cups flour
1	tablespoon baking powder
1	cup chocolate chips
1	cup pecans or walnuts, chopped

Preheat oven to 350 degrees. Grease a 9x13" pan and set aside.

In a large saucepan, melt the margarine. Remove from heat and stir in the sugar, mixing until the sugar has absorbed all the margarine.

Add the cocoa, then stir in the vanilla and salt. Mix well.

Beat in the eggs, one at a time. Add the flour, baking powder, chocolate chips and the nuts.

Spread into prepared pan. Bake 30 to 35 minutes.
Yield: 18 to 24

Hints
These brownies are more "fudgy" and less "caky" than most.
They will rise during baking, then fall when removed from the oven.

Angel Food Cake
by Joanna Wolfe

2	cups sugar
1 1/2	cups cake flour
12	egg whites at room temperature
1/2	teaspoon salt
1 1/2	teaspoons cream of tartar
1/2	teaspoon pure almond extract
1	teaspoon vanilla

Preheat oven to 325 degrees.

In a bowl, sift together TWICE 1 cup of the sugar with the cake flour and set aside.

In a very large bowl, beat the egg whites until foamy, using a flat whisk. Add the salt and beat again. Then add the cream of tartar and beat until mixture forms soft peaks.

While continuing to beat the egg mixture, spoon in the remaining cup of sugar, a spoonful at a time. Mixture should begin to turn glossy and peaks should stiffen.

Sift again the flour and sugar you have set aside. Then, sift once more into the beaten mixture, a spoonful at a time. Fold ingredients together gently and do not beat. Fold in almond extract and vanilla.

Pour into an angel food cake pan and place in center of oven. Bake for 60 to 75 minutes, or until golden brown. When cake is done, remove from oven and invert over a cooling rack (this prevents cake from collapsing). Let cool overnight.

The next day, run a flat spatula around the edges to loosen cake and remove from pan.

Yield: 12 to 16 servings

Hints

DO NOT grease pan; it will make the egg whites fall.

Use an angel food cake pan with legs and removable bottom.

This is a good way to use up old eggs — they actually work better than fresh ones!

Joanna suggests having a "helper" to sift and add ingredients while you beat the eggs.

Do not use a mixer; it "mixes down" and you want to "whip up."

Scottish Shortbread
by Joanna Wolfe

   3   cups flour
   2   cups butter, softened
   1   cup confectioners sugar

Preheat oven to 350 degrees.

Blend all ingredients together with a fork or with your fingers. Press into a 9x13" pan. Bake until light brown, about 15 minutes, but watch carefully to avoid overbrowning.

Remove from oven and cut into squares or bars while still warm.

Yield: 3 dozen

Hints

Use a pizza cutter to slice the shortbread.

Unlike most cookies, this recipe contains no leavening ingredients, so you can double or triple it as long as you maintain the proportions.

Cameron

Betty Reitzel

To find Cameron, you have to be looking for it. Go too far on U.S. 1 and you'll miss the turnoff leading to this little town of Victorian antique shops. Cross the railroad tracks on the highway too fast and you'll pass it altogether.

But if you slow down, take your time, look around for a while....

Betty Reitzel's house sits back from the road, on 20 acres outside of town, with a view of gently rolling hills all around. Even on this dreary spring day, Betty's kitchen is a sunny place to spend the afternoon.

She's been busy. On the table are Rocky Road brownies, chocolate chip cookies, raisin-bran muffins, bread and Russian tea. That's just a sample of what Betty can do.

Leaf through the Cameron Presbyterian Church cookbook; you'll see Betty's name on almost every page. She contributed nearly 100 recipes, and the book is now in its third printing.

"Mother never let me in the kitchen," says Betty, a Massachusetts native. She had four sisters, and if her mother let them all in the kitchen, it was too crowded to cook. So Betty didn't learn her way around the culinary world until she was married.

"If you can read, you can cook," Betty believes.

When she married Raymond Reitzel, she claims, she "couldn't even make coffee."

So Betty picked up a cookbook — one she'd gotten as a gift for her bridal registry at a department store — and taught herself how. Raymond gained 30 pounds in six months.

Betty's the first to admit to a lifelong competitive streak, so when she saw that a neighbor had entered a local county fair, she couldn't resist. From there, it was on to the State Fair.

People come to Cameron's street festival from great distances to line up at Betty's table for the goodies she offers for sale. She's been known to bake 500 cookies, plus dozens of cakes and breads, beating the batter for all by hand.

"You're not going to do this anymore," Raymond grumbled once.

"You're right, Honey," Betty agreed. "Absolutely."

She laughs. "But every year, here we are!"

...So if it's the first weekend in May, take your foot off the gas in

When Betty Reitzel isn't busy in the kitchen, she creates beautiful one-of-a-kind baskets.

Cameron and roll your window down. Chances are good you'll be able to smell Betty Reitzel's cream cheese tarts all the way up Carthage Street.

Cinnamon Bread
by Betty Reitzel

    1   tablespoon cinnamon
    1   cup + 3 tablespoons sugar
    2   cups flour
    1   teaspoon baking powder
1/2   teaspoon baking soda
       dash of salt
1/4   cup shortening
    2   eggs
    1   cup sour milk
    1   teaspoon vanilla

Preheat oven to 350 degrees. Grease a 5x9" loaf pan and set aside.

In a small bowl, combine 3 tablespoons of the sugar and the cinnamon. Set aside.

Combine flour, baking powder, baking soda and salt.

In another bowl, cream shortening; gradually add the remaining 1 cup sugar. Add eggs to the creamed mixture, one at a time, and beat until well blended.

Add flour mixture to the creamed ingredients alternately with the milk. Beat well after each addition. Stir in vanilla.

Spoon half of batter into prepared pan. Sprinkle with half of the cinnamon-sugar mixture. Cover with remaining batter and top with the rest of the cinnamon-sugar.

Bake for 40 to 50 minutes, or until a tester inserted into the center comes out clean.

Yield: 1 loaf

Hint

To "sour" milk, stir 1 tablespoon lemon juice or white vinegar into 1 cup of milk.

Raisin-Bran Muffins
by Betty Reitzel

3	cups bran cereal
1	cup boiling water
1/2	cup oil
2 1/2	cups flour
1	teaspoon salt
1 1/2	cups sugar
2 1/2	teaspoons baking soda
2	eggs, beaten
2	cups milk
1	cup raisins

Preheat oven to 400 degrees. Grease a muffin tin or place paper liners in cups and set aside.

Combine 1 cup bran cereal, boiling water and oil. Mix well and set aside.

In another bowl, mix flour, salt, sugar, baking soda and the other 2 cups of cereal. Add the eggs, then the milk and stir until well-blended. Then add the cereal-oil mixture. Stir in raisins.

Spoon batter into muffin tins, filling each about 2/3 full. Bake for 15 to 20 minutes, or until muffins begin to pull away from the sides of the tin. Remove from oven and turn out of pans to cool.

Yield: About 30.

Hints

These are best served hot.
Betty says this batter will keep, covered in the refrigerator, for a month.
You may use buttermilk in this recipe.

One-Bowl Eggless Chocolate Cake by Betty Reitzel

1 1/2	cups flour
1 1/4	cups sugar
3	tablespoons cocoa
1	teaspoon baking soda
1/2	teaspoon salt
6	tablespoons oil
1	tablespoon vinegar
1	teaspoon vanilla
1	cup cold water

Preheat oven to 375 degrees. Line a 9x9" pan with wax paper and set aside.

Into a bowl, sift together the flour, sugar, cocoa, baking soda, and salt. With a spoon, make 3 "holes" in the dry ingredients. Pour oil into the first, vinegar into the second and vanilla into the third. Then pour the water into the bowl and mix well. Pour into a pan and bake for 35 to 40 minutes or until a toothpick inserted into cake comes out clean.

Yield: 8 to 12 servings

Hint

Betty likes the moistness of this cake.

Irish Soda Bread
by Betty Reitzel's sister, Alice Duggan

The batter:
   2 cups milk
   2 tablespoons vinegar
   4 cups flour
1/2 cup sugar
1/2 teaspoon salt
   1 teaspoon baking soda
   2 teaspoons baking powder
   1 tablespoon margarine
   2 teaspoons caraway seeds
   1 cup raisins

The topping:
2 1/2 tablespoons sugar
   1 tablespoon margarine, melted

Preheat oven to 375 degrees. Grease a 9" loaf pan or 2 1-pound coffee tins. Set aside.

Combine milk and vinegar. Set aside.

Mix dry ingredients into a bowl. Add 1 tablespoon margarine (not melted), caraway seeds and raisins. Stir until blended. Add milk mixture. Stir until thoroughly mixed.

Pour into prepared pan or pans. Drizzle with melted margarine and sprinkle with sugar.

Bake at 375 degrees for 10 minutes, then reduce heat to 350 degrees and bake for 50 minutes, or until brown.

Yield: 1 9" loaf or 2 smaller loaves

Hint
Caraway seeds may be omitted.

Blueberry Tea Cake
by Betty Reitzel's sister, Alice Duggan

1 1/2	cups flour
1	teaspoon baking powder
1/4	teaspoon salt
1/2	cup margarine
1	cup sugar
2	eggs
1/3	cup milk
1 1/2-1 3/4	cups blueberries, floured*
1	teaspoon vanilla
	Grated nutmeg and sugar to sprinkle on top

Preheat oven to 350 degrees. Grease an 8x8" pan and set aside.

Sift together the flour, baking powder and salt; set aside.

In another bowl, cream together the margarine and sugar. To this, add the eggs and mix well. Then add the dry ingredients alternately with the milk, beating well. Stir in vanilla, then fold in berries.

Pour batter into prepared pan. Sprinkle with sugar and nutmeg. Bake for 35 to 40 minutes, or until a toothpick inserted into cake comes out clean.

Yield: 8 servings

Hints

To "flour" blueberries: wash and dry thoroughly. Place berries in a large plastic bag or container. Sprinkle with several tablespoons of flour and shake gently to coat. This keeps the blueberries from "sinking" to the bottom of the pan.

Try "floured" berries in muffins, too.

Easy No-Bake Fruit Cake
by Betty Reitzel

```
      1  cup evaporated milk
    1/2  cup water
      2  boxes graham cracker crumbs
      2  teaspoons cinnamon
      2  teaspoons nutmeg
      1  teaspoon ground cloves
      3  cups raisins, seedless
  1 1/2  cups walnuts or pecans, broken
    1/2  cup dates, finely chopped
  2 1/2  cups diced candied fruit and peel (made for fruitcake)
           Candied fruits and nut halves for garnish (optional)
```

Line 2 5x9" loaf pans with wax paper. Set aside.

In a small bowl or measuring cup, mix together milk and water.

In a very large bowl, combine crumbs, cinnamon, nutmeg, cloves, raisins, nuts and fruits. Add milk mixture. Knead until dough is uniformly moistened. Press firmly into lined pans.

Garnish with nut halves or candied fruits if desired. Cover tightly and refrigerate 2 to 3 days to allow flavors to blend. Store in refrigerator.

Yield: 2 5x9" loaves

Baklava
by Betty Reitzel

The syrup:
```
  2 1/2  cups sugar
  1 1/4  cups water
      1  teaspoon fresh lemon juice
  1 1/2  tablespoons honey
```

Combine above ingredients in a saucepan and bring to a boil. Simmer 1 minute. Remove from heat and allow to stand at least 5 minutes before spooning over warm pastry.

The filling:
>   2   cups walnuts, finely chopped
>   3   tablespoons sugar
>   1   teaspoon cinnamon

Combine filling ingredients and mix well.

To assemble the baklava:
3/4 to 1   pound unsalted butter, melted
>   1   pound fillo dough

Preheat oven to 350 degrees. Butter a 9x13" pan. One at a time, layer 5 sheets of fillo into the pan. Brush top sheet with melted butter.

Place another 5 sheets in the pan, one at a time; brush top sheet with butter. Repeat, using 3 sheets of dough, brushing the top sheet with butter.

Spread walnut filling evenly across the dough in pan. Layer 5 sheets of fillo, one at a time, on top of the filling. Brush top sheet with butter. Repeat until pan is full. Brush top with butter.

Before baking, cut through all the layers on the diagonal with a sharp knife, making a diamond pattern. Bake for 20 to 30 minutes or until golden brown.

Remove from oven and allow to cool slightly. Spoon syrup over top.

Yield: About 4 dozen

Hints

Most grocery stores now carry fillo dough in the freezer section. Defrost before using.

Fillo dries out quickly; here's how to keep it pliable:

Unwrap the package and place the defrosted sheets on a towel near your work surface.

Cover with plastic wrap.

Place another slightly damp towel on top of the plastic.

Every time you remove a sheet to use, cover the others.

Apple Dumplings
by Betty Reitzel

      2   cups sugar
      2   cups water
    1/4   teaspoon cinnamon
    1/4   teaspoon nutmeg
    1/2   cup butter
      2   cups flour
    3/4   teaspoon salt
      2   teaspoons baking powder
  3/4-1   cup shortening
    1/2   cup milk
      6   small apples, peeled and cored
          Additional sugar and cinnamon to sprinkle on top
          Butter

Preheat oven to 375 degrees. Grease 1 large or 2 medium baking dishes. Set aside.

For the sauce:
In a saucepan, combine sugar, water, cinnamon and nutmeg. Bring to a boil, reduce heat and simmer 5 minutes. Remove from heat and stir in butter.

For the dumplings:
In a bowl, sift together flour, salt and baking powder. Blend in shortening. Add milk and stir only until moistened.

On a floured surface, roll dough to 1/4" thick. Cut into 6 equal squares.

Place one apple in center of each square. Sprinkle with sugar and cinnamon; dot with butter. Grasp corners of dough and bring up to meet in center, covering apple each apple completely. Pinch edges to seal. Place dumplings at least 1" from each other in the baking dish. Pour sauce over dumplings.

Bake for 45 minutes, basting several times. Serve warm.
Yield: 6

Liver Treats for Dogs
by Betty Reitzel

    1   pound liver
    2   eggs
  3/4   cup cornmeal
  1/2   cup milk
  1/2   cup wheat germ
         Whole wheat flour

Preheat oven to 325 degrees. Grease a 9x13" or jelly roll pan. Set aside.

Place liver in blender or food processor. Grind. Add eggs, cornmeal, milk and wheat germ.

Add enough whole wheat flour to make a dough that looks like brownie batter. Spread in pan. Bake 35 to 40 minutes until toothpick inserted comes out clean.

Remove from oven, cool and cut into squares. Keep refrigerated in plastic wrap.

Yield: 2 to 3 dozen

Hints

Open the windows while baking — your dog will love you, but your family may not.

Label the bag in your fridge!

Wendell

Joy Alford

She had worked extra-hard on her school project, an American flag she made out of canvas, and she had been disappointed when the teacher gave her a low grade. But Joy knew her work was good. So she entered the flag in the State Fair.

It won a blue ribbon.

Moments like those are too rare for Joy Alford. She's the first to admit she's not a very good student. Academics are not where she shines, but it isn't for lack of trying. Joy has had to work extra hard, just to try to keep up with her classmates.

Fortunately, her parents understand. Stan and Edna Alford encourage Joy, who's 17, and her little sister, Hope, to express themselves in the ways they know best: through painting and sewing, cake decorating and baking. It was a local 4-H chapter that helped give Joy her start, but from there the accomplishments have been hers alone.

She keeps a loose-leaf notebook of her favorite recipes, some from family members and some she's tried on her own. She's won several dozen ribbons, and each success spurs her to take the next step.

Joy's mother thinks entering the State Fair is "fantastic," especially for young people who may need a little help developing self-confidence. She remembers when Joy wanted to create a decorated cake in the design of a horse.

"Joy, that's too hard," Edna said, knowing her daughter was just a beginner.

Joy was determined. "I want to do it and I'm going to do it," she insisted.

The cake, like Joy's flag from school, was awarded the blue ribbon.

"It never hurts to try," she says, with a shy smile.

Stan's mother was an artist, too, and the Alfords believe it was her talent that Joy inherited. That talent continues to inspire today: A portrait of Jesus, painted by Joy's grandmother when she was 16 years old, hangs proudly in the Alfords' home. It's a daily reminder of what matters most in their lives.

There's a quiet kind of richness to the way the Alfords live. Most everything they need is within reach, though they're miles from the

Little sister Hope sits on the lap of her big sister, Joy Alford. Both prize-winners are learning to compete and win while having fun.

nearest mall or fast food. Chickens give the family fresh eggs for cooking and baking, and three country stores are just down the road.

Resisting the trend of some families to move to the city, Edna says, "We wanted our kids to be able to grow up the way we did." She points toward town, then in the opposite direction: "There are seven families of our relatives living here on Grandaddy's land."

Joy Alford personifies learning that comes about in a different way. In an environment of support and guidance, she is exploring her own abilities. Her parents are learning, too — to recognize their daughter's uniqueness and to celebrate her success. And while she knows there will be obstacles ahead, Joy has no doubt she will make her own way in the world.

One-Bowl Rocky Road Brownies
by Joy Alford

    4   squares unsweetened chocolate
  3/4   cup margarine
    2   cups sugar
    3   eggs
    1   teaspoon vanilla
    1   cup all-purpose flour
1 1/2   cups coarsely chopped nuts
    2   cups miniature marshmallows
    1   cup semi-sweet chocolate chips

Preheat oven to 350 degrees. Grease a 9x13" pan and set aside.
In a large saucepan on low heat, melt together the unsweetened chocolate and margarine. (Or, microwave on "high" in a microwave-safe bowl for 2 minutes. Stir and reheat briefly if needed to melt margarine.)
Stir in sugar, then eggs and vanilla. Mix in flour and 3/4 cup nuts. Spread into pan and bake for 35 minutes. Remove from oven and immediately sprinkle with marshmallows, chocolate chips and remaining nuts. Return to oven and bake 3 minutes, or until toppings begin to melt.
Cool in pan before slicing into squares.
Yield: 2 dozen

Honey Crunch Cookies
by Joy Alford

  1/2   cup butter
  1/2   cup sugar
  1/2   cup honey
    1   egg, beaten
    1   teaspoon vanilla
    1   cup flour
  1/2   teaspoon baking soda
  1/2   teaspoon baking powder
  1/4   teaspoon salt
    1   cup oatmeal, uncooked
    1   cup shredded coconut
  1/2   cup walnuts or pecans, chopped

Preheat oven to 350 degrees. Grease a cookie sheet and set aside.

In a bowl, combine butter, sugar and honey. Beat well. Add egg and vanilla.

In a separate bowl, stir together the flour, baking soda, baking powder and salt. Add to the butter mixture and stir until well-blended. Stir in the oatmeal, coconut and nuts.

Drop by rounded teaspoonfuls onto prepared cookie sheet about 2" apart. Bake 10 to 12 minutes or until golden brown.

Remove cookies carefully from sheet and allow to cool on wire rack.
Yield: 2 1/2 to 3 dozen

Hint
These are crunchy when they come out of the oven. They become chewier as they cool. If you like them crisper, reheat briefly before serving.

Each year, hundreds of entries are submitted in the baked goods competitions at the North Carolina State Fair.

King
Susan and Harvey Moser

From the top of Pilot Mountain, Highway 52 is a gray ribbon threading through the little green towns below. A few miles down the road lies King, a place where the main street is called Main Street, and the drug store still serves fountain Cokes.

Susan Moser has lived in King for more than 20 years, in the same house her husband, Harvey, built when the two were first married. Growing up in nearby Rural Hall, Susan went with her friends to the Tiny Diny and the Dairy-O — that's where Harvey first set his sights on her. After they married and began putting down roots, they decided they wanted to be more self-sufficient and began gardening, canning and preserving.

"It's a lifestyle for us," Harvey says.

That lifestyle led to a success in competition they never imagined.

"We stopped counting ribbons at 549," says Susan.

Yes, 549. A walk through their garden explains it all. The colors and varieties of flowers, herbs and vegetables are endless. Red, yellow, green; orange, purple and lilac — those are just the peppers. There are striped eggplants, black pansies, and red carrots, too. A hothouse holds seed-starting trays, with each single sprout carefully labeled.

Planning their organic garden is a year-round project for Harvey and Susan. They like to try new things, so each winter they order seeds that strike their fancy from catalogs. Come fall, you'll find the Mosers entering their harvest at the Stokes County Fair, the Surry County Fair, the Dixie Classic Fair in Winston-Salem, and, of course, the State Fair.

In any competition, there are always stories of things that go wrong. One year, early on, the Mosers planted their onions a little too close to the creek. A heavy rain tore the plants loose and washed them away. Neighbors reported seeing those uprooted onions come floating down the creek a mile away.

As the conversation turns to baking, the Mosers share some hints that have helped them win.

Susan's Pecan Shortbread cookies and pound cakes are her blue-ribbon winners.

"I've been baking ever since my mama first sat me up in a chair and let me hold the mixer," she says. "I love my Kitchen-aid. It really does

Harvey and Susan Moser lost count of their ribbons somewhere around 500.

make a difference, especially with cakes."

And the secret to perfect pie crust?

"You won't want to hear this," Harvey says, grinning. "It's lard. For biscuits, too."

Their rivalry is good-natured. "Fair people, they're like a family," Susan says.

Once, the Mosers "accused" a fellow entrant of setting raccoons loose in their garden to devour a prized crop. Then there was the time Harvey discovered that the "nice man" who always helped Susan unload her entries was the same fellow who had been beating Harvey time after time.

"We learn something every year," Harvey says. "There's nothing better than to plant something new and watch it as it grows."

And what do they do with all those eggplants and beans and tomatoes?

"We give a lot away," Harvey says. "The good Lord gives us a good crop, and we share with other people."

"The hand that gives, gets," adds Susan.

Susan and Harvey Moser's Hints for Gardening

Use bone meal in your garden. It helps root development and makes vegetables sweeter.

For seeds that have a hard casing (like beets, carrots and spinach) try soaking them overnight in a glass of tea. They'll germinate more easily.

Molded Mints by Susan Moser

2	tablespoons softened butter
2	tablespoons shortening
2	tablespoons warm water
2 1/2	cups confectioners sugar
10	drops peppermint extract

Cream butter and shortening together. Stir in peppermint oil. Add water and 2 cups of confectioners sugar. Stir in peppermint extract. Mix until smooth.

Begin adding remaining sugar, mixing with your hands, only until mixture becomes moldable.

Press into rubber molds, or pat out and cut into shapes using small cutters. Refrigerate.

Yield: 4 to 6 dozen, depending on size

Hint
Fun for kids to make. Try adding different food colorings.

Pecan Shortbread Cookies
by Susan Moser

  1   cup butter, softened
1/2 cup confectioners sugar
  2   teaspoons vanilla
  1   tablespoon water
  2   cups flour
  1   cup chopped pecans
      confectioners sugar for dusting

The day before baking the cookies:
Cream together the butter and sugar. Add vanilla, water, flour and pecans, mixing well after each addition.

Cover and chill in refrigerator overnight.

The next day:
Preheat oven to 325 degrees. Lightly grease a cookie sheet and set aside.

Roll dough into balls 1" in diameter. Place on cookie sheet, leaving at least 1" between each, and press flat. Bake 15 to 20 minutes or until light golden brown.

While cookies are still warm, dust with additional confectioners sugar.

Yield: 3 to 4 dozen

Italian Cream Cake
by Susan Moser

1/2 cup butter or margarine, softened
1/2 cup shortening
  2   cups sugar
  5   eggs, separated
  2   cups all-purpose flour
  1   teaspoon baking soda
  1   cup buttermilk
  1   teaspoon vanilla
3/4 cup chopped walnuts
3/4 cup coconut

Preheat oven to 350 degrees. Grease and flour 3 9" cake pans. Set aside.

Cream together butter, shortening and sugar until fluffy. Add egg yolks and beat until well-blended.

Beat egg whites until soft peaks form. Set aside.

In a separate bowl, sift together flour and baking soda. Alternately add flour mixture and buttermilk to the creamed mixture, blending well after each addition. Stir in vanilla, then the chopped nuts and coconut.

Fold in beaten egg whites. Pour into prepared pans. Bake for 20 minutes, or until a tester inserted into the center of cake comes out clean.

Cool and remove from pans. Frost between layers, on top and on sides with Cream Cheese Walnut Frosting.

Yield: 12 to 16 servings

Hint
This cake should be refrigerated.

Cream Cheese Walnut Frosting
by Susan Moser

8 oz. cream cheese, softened
1/2 cup butter or margarine, softened
1/4 cup chopped walnuts
1 teaspoon vanilla
1 box confectioners sugar

Beat all ingredients together until well-blended. Spread on cooled cake.

Yield: About 1 1/2 cups

Hint
Adding chopped nuts to frosting can help hide crumbs that come loose while you are spreading the frosting.

Applesauce Pound Cake
by Susan Moser

3	cups all-purpose flour
2	teaspoons baking soda
1/2	teaspoon salt
1 1/2	teaspoons cinnamon
1/2	teaspoon allspice
1	cup margarine or butter, softened
1	cup light brown sugar, packed
1	cup granulated sugar
1	egg
2	cups applesauce
3/4	cup raisins
3/4	cup chopped pecans

Preheat oven to 350 degrees. Grease and flour a 10" tube pan.

Sift together flour, soda, salt and spices. Set aside.

In a large bowl, cream together the butter, both sugars and egg until fluffy. Alternately add the applesauce and the flour mixture. Beat until well-blended. Stir in raisins and pecans.

Pour batter into prepared pan. Bake 65 to 75 minutes, or until a tester inserted into the center of cake comes out clean.

Cool in pan for 15 minutes, invert onto serving plate.

Yield: 12 to 16 servings

Hint
This makes a nice change from fruitcake at Christmas time.

Pumpkin Walnut Pound Cake
by Susan Moser

3	cups all-purpose flour
2	teaspoons baking powder
2	teaspoons baking soda
1	teaspoon salt
2 1/4	teaspoons cinnamon
1/2	teaspoon allspice
2	cups sugar
4	eggs, beaten
1 1/2	cups corn oil
2	cups pumpkin, canned or cooked and mashed
3/4	cup chopped walnuts

Preheat oven to 350 degrees. Grease and flour a 10" tube pan. Set aside.

Into a large bowl, sift together the flour, baking powder, baking soda, salt, cinnamon, allspice and sugar. Make a "well" in the center.

Add beaten eggs, corn oil and pumpkin. Beat until smooth. Stir in walnuts.

Pour into prepared pan. Bake 65 to 70 minutes, or until a tester inserted into the center of cake comes out clean.

Cool in pan for 15 minutes, invert onto serving plate.

Yield: 12 to 16 servings

Morrisville

Carolyn Leverett

The cow had lain down near the creek to deliver her calf, but something was wrong. She was tired from hours of pushing, and the calf would die if it wasn't born soon.

Carolyn crept up slowly and quietly, not wanting to frighten the laboring animal. The calf's front hooves had begun to emerge. When the mother pushed, the young woman pulled, keeping her head low. Then they both rested. Then more pushing, more pulling.

The calf was born.

The mother was too weak to clean her newborn baby, so Carolyn wiped his muzzle to start his breathing.

Carolyn Leverett is 14 years old.

The springtime sky above the Leverett family farm seems a little bluer than back in the city. Carolyn and her mom, Debbie, are explaining what it takes to keep up with their 112 acres.

"We've got to get the hay up," Carolyn says, then describes each step of the summer ritual to come: "Cutting, turning, fluffing, drying, raking and baling."

She and her three brothers will take turns driving the tractor, then throwing and stacking the bales.

Farm days are long ones. Even today, most chores are done the old way, by hand and on a schedule.

Here is Carolyn's typical day: She wakes early, shares breakfast and family devotions with her parents and brothers. Private devotions follow, then Carolyn begins tending to her goats and sheep. Hauling water, feeding and exercising the animals will take an hour or more. Shortly after 9:00, her school lessons begin.

Afternoons, she bakes for the family and again tends to her animals, accepting freely her responsibilities and routine.

Her parents, Charlie and Debbie Leverett, have chosen to home school their children — Chris, Stephen, Philip and Carolyn.

"Not only are we to teach our children in the ways of the Lord, but we should teach them all aspects of life from a Christian perspective," Debbie explains.

The Leverett boys are industrious, chopping and selling firewood. With the money they earned two Christmases ago, the family poured

Farm days are busy for Carolyn Leverett, who makes time for baking when chores are finished.

their own backyard basketball court, complete with lights. Debbie and her daughter laugh, recalling games that went on into the night. Working hard means you can play hard, too.

Her rubber boots squishing through the mud along the fence, Carolyn poses for a photograph with her prize-winning lamb, "Lamborghini." She enjoys keeping show and prize records, and today she's demonstrating how she converted the old chicken house into pens with removable gates for her goats.

Her success showing livestock at the State Fair is shaping her future. "I want to work with large animals," she says decisively.

Carolyn entered her pumpkin muffins for the first time in 1994 and won a blue ribbon. Like many teenagers, she doesn't profess any secrets to success, only a willingness to try. But Debbie thinks the homemade apple cider they use in baking makes a difference.

The Leveretts are grateful to have family nearby — Debbie's parents are in Durham, and Charlie's live just down the road in another house on the farm. Together, the family is renovating their 100-year-old home. It's a learning experience.

"This place has a lot of memories," Debbie says. "At one time, we had four generations living here on the farm."

The Leveretts don't think their lifestyle is unusual. "All this is a gift," Debbie says emphatically.

Carolyn checks the latch on the gate before she walks back to the house with her mother. Each animal has been cared for, each pen has been cleaned. Next year's fair is months away, but Carolyn is well on her way to another successful season.

Pumpkin Muffins
by Carolyn Leverett

16 oz.	cooked pumpkin
2	cups light brown sugar
1	cup margarine
4	eggs
1/2	cup apple cider
3 1/2	cups unbleached flour
2	teaspoons baking soda
1	teaspoon salt
4 1/2	teaspoons cinnamon
1/2	teaspoon cloves
2	teaspoons baking powder
4 1/2	teaspoons ground ginger
1	teaspoon nutmeg

Preheat oven to 350 degrees. Grease a muffin tin and set aside.

Stir together the pumpkin, sugar and margarine. Add eggs and beat until smooth. Stir in the cider. Set aside.

Sift dry ingredients into bowl. Gradually add the pumpkin mixture to the dry ingredients and mix until blended. Spoon batter into muffin tins, about 2/3 full.

Bake for 20 minutes or until an inserted toothpick comes out clean.
Yield: About 20 muffins

Hint
These muffins are spicy and flavorful. Carolyn's homemade cider makes them extra-good, but store bought cider is fine, too.

Easy Cream Cheese Lemon Bars
by Carolyn Leverett

	One box lemon cake mix*
1/2	cup margarine, melted
3	eggs, one slightly beaten
	One box of lemon frosting mix (not pre-mixed frosting) OR
	One box vanilla frosting mix + 1 teaspoon lemon extract
8 oz.	cream cheese, softened

Preheat oven to 350. Grease a 9x13" pan on bottom only. Set aside.

Combine cake mix, margarine and 1 beaten egg. Mix with fork until moistened. Pat into pan.

Blend lemon frosting mix (or vanilla frosting and lemon extract) into cream cheese. Set aside 1/2 cup of this mixture; it will be used to frost the baked bars.

Add the other 2 eggs to the remaining frosting mixture. Beat 3 to 5 minutes and spread over cake mixture in pan.

Bake for 30 to 40 minutes. Cool and spread with reserved frosting.

Yield: 12 to 24 bars, depending on size

Hint
Junior division bakers are allowed to use packaged mixes as a base for recipes. This is a good way for younger bakers to learn kitchen skills with a project almost guaranteed to turn out well.

Raleigh

Dee Pufpaff

Her family were true Cajuns — the French who settled in Acadia, then migrated south from Nova Scotia to Louisiana. But Dee Pufpaff's journeys have taken her farther than her ancestors could ever have imagined. Here is her story in her own words:

"I'm Deborah Ann Victoria DuPont Pufpaff. I was born in 'Morevill,' Louisiana. And I lived in Big Bend. No. Spell that M-O-R-E-A-U-V-I-L-L-E — Moreauville, Louisiana.

"My grandmother still lives in Big Bend. She taught me how to make biscuits for 4-H when I was nine. Well, I won, and she let me make biscuits every Saturday after that. She'll be 80 years old March 9th. We've offered her to come up here and visit, but she says, 'Oh, no, honey.' I don't think but maybe one time she's ever been out of the state of Louisiana.

"I still remember my grandfather — I called him 'Paw-Paw' — who died when I was seven years old. We'd go across the road to get the cows and bring them in for milking. We had this one old brown-and-black cow who was so gentle. He'd put me on her, and I'd ride to the barn on that cow. She was as slow as next week.

"My family made boudin sausage — there's a white and a red kind — and they'd send me off so I wouldn't be too distressed when they went out there with the guns. Let me tell you, you get a real good respect for meat. When my grandfather died, my grandmother sold most of the animals.

"Now, I like to tell my daughter, Mattie, stories about those days, instead of those bedtime things, you know? My grandmother would always tell us, 'No, no — you don't speak French — you speak English.' Back then they only went as far as the sixth grade, then you went to work in the fields.

"She made fried dough, something like what they call 'beignets' now, only we called them 'crepes.' We'd have them Saturday mornings with butter and syrup. I can remember looking down the table and there'd be seven cakes that my grandmother had baked all day. Peanut butter and chocolate and pineapple and coconut. Well, one time, somehow the cat got in the house while we were outside doing chores. And that cat was sitting on the table and was taking one bite out of

Dee Pufpaff serves "morning tea," a custom her family enjoyed when they lived in Australia.

every one of those cakes!

"That place, it's kind of lost in time. Now, the young kids when they grow up, they move off to the cities because there's nothing there. No job opportunities.

"For me, cooking just comes natural. I never had spaghetti growing up. I didn't know what it was. And where I come from, we don't put tomatoes in our gumbo. We use the gumbo file (fee-lay) seasoning and that's it. It's kind of green. The only thing I know where we put tomatoes is in okra stew.

"I believe in those old iron skillets. I've got eight of them. Two or three belonged to my husband Mike's grandmother. I have one just for bread. See this one? It's as slick as a baby's bottom. Never cook meat or potatoes or anything else in a bread skillet. It absorbs the odor.

"Here's how to cure a skillet. Wash it, grease it, then put it in the sun, outside in the summertime when it's hot. Let it sit in the sun. Bring it in, wash it, grease it again, put it in the oven for the night.

Next day, do it all again. Keep doing that till you get it right.

"I start thinking in July about the State Fair in October. I like *Country Woman* magazine and *Taste of Home.* I'll look at a recipe in one of those and think, 'You know, I'll bet if I add this or that it will really make it good.'

"Mike works for Northern Telecom and for Bell. We lived in Australia for two years. The first year was really tough, just adjusting. I had a real time getting my cooking to turn out. The ingredients are just different. They don't use a lot of preservatives. Where we feed our cattle on grain, theirs graze on grass. So the meat even smells and tastes different. And the temperatures are in Celsius. The measurements, too, so you need a little chart.

"The second year Mattie felt more accepted at school. I was helping, making morning tea for the teachers — that's something they do over there at least once a week. After breakfast, about nine, ten o'clock. Mostly pastries, sometimes little sandwiches. The teachers even gave me an award, just for doing it. I love that custom.

"The stores? They're not like a grocery store here. In Australia, you've got big malls with department stores, plus they have food stores. You've got the fruit market, the fish market, then there's the bread store — all in the mall. It's wonderful.

"Here, we're so rushed to death. In Australia, things close up about 4:00 in the afternoon. Even most grocery stores. They really believe in family life.

"Not only were the scenery and the landscape different, but the people and the accents, too. But it's just like in Louisiana — people will always have names for others who are different. But I think it makes life more interesting. I like it. I'd do it again. My feet are itching."

Asked what she believes to be important, Dee replies, "Well, my grandmother taught us to believe in these things: loyalty, honor, tradition, family. And she said, 'Always cook an extra chicken leg in case someone drops in.'"

Lady Lamingtons
by Dee Pufpaff

1	pound cake or square cake, baked and cooled
1/3	cup hot water
2	tablespoons butter, cut into pieces for easier melting
1/4	cup cocoa
2 1/2	cups confectioners sugar
2 1/2	cups extra-fine grated coconut

Cut cake into approximately 20 rectangles using a serrated knife. In a bowl whisk together hot water, butter and cocoa until dissolved. Using a wooden spoon, mix in the sugar. If mixture is too thick for dipping, add a little hot water.

Holding the pieces of cake with a fork, dip each one into the mixture to coat lightly, then roll in coconut. Place on wax paper to cool. Keep in refrigerator.

Yield: About 20

Hints

These are named after Lady Lamington, whose husband was Governor of Queensland, Australia.

These are easy to make and elegant to serve.

Skillet Cornbread
by Dee Pufpaff

1	cup all-purpose flour
1	cup yellow cornmeal
1/3	cup sugar
4	teaspoons baking powder
1/2	teaspoon salt
1 1/4	cups milk, room temperature
1/3	cup oil
2	eggs, beaten

Oil a 10" iron skillet and place in a cold oven. Preheat to 400 degrees for at least 10 minutes.

Mix all ingredients together until blended. Remove skillet from oven, pour in batter and return to oven. Bake for 25 minutes or until golden brown.

Yield: 8 to 10 servings

Hints

When pouring the batter into the skillet, the edges should begin to curl up and cook. If not, your skillet wasn't hot enough.

In Dee's family, this was served hot with butter and syrup.

She likes the House-Autry brand of cornmeal.

Crepes (Beignets)
by Dee Pufpaff

1/2	cup warm (not hot) water, about 115 degrees
2	packages dry yeast
3/4	cup lukewarm milk
1/2	cup sugar
2	teaspoons salt
1/4	cup shortening
2	eggs
5	cups all-purpose flour
	Peanut oil for frying

Sprinkle yeast into the warm water and stir. Set aside for 5 minutes.

Combine warm milk, sugar and salt in a large bowl. Stir to dissolve. Using a mixer, beat in shortening, eggs, yeast mixture and 2 cups of flour until smooth.

Add remaining flour and mix until dough leaves the sides of the bowl. Turn out onto a lightly floured board and knead until smooth, elastic — and no longer sticky. Place in a lightly greased bowl and cover with a clean cloth or towel. Let rise in a warm place, away from drafts, until doubled in size, about an hour.

Punch down. Divide dough into two equal portions. (At this point, one half may be frozen for later use.)

Fill a large iron skillet halfway with oil. Heat over medium flame, but do not allow oil to smoke. Pinch off flat pieces of dough about 2" in diameter and lower into the hot oil. Do not crowd. Turn to brown evenly on both sides. Remove and drain on paper towels.

Serve with jam and confectioners sugar or butter and syrup.
Yield: About 2 dozen

Hints

These Louisiana-style "crepes" are not the filled flat pancakes. They are more like what are called beignets in New Orleans.

You can prepare the dough the night before and place in a cold oven to rise overnight. The next morning, punch down the dough and you're ready to cook the crepes.

Dee not only remembers these fondly from her own childhood, she says her daughter, Mattie, loves them too. A hit with kids!

Peanut oil is recommended because it can be heated to a higher temperature than most oils, without smoking.

Do not crowd crepes in pan.

Cherries in the Snow
by Dee Pufpaff

1	angel food or pound cake, baked
1/2	cup sugar
1/2	cup milk
8 oz.	cream cheese
16 oz.	frozen dessert topping
3-4	cups homemade OR 2 cans prepared cherry pie filling

Mix milk, sugar and cream cheese together until creamy. Fold in dessert topping. Break up cake into bite-sized pieces and fold into mixture.

Spoon mixture into a trifle or other glass bowl. Pack firmly. Pour cherries over top. Refrigerate overnight to allow cherries to soak through the layers.
Yield: 12 to 16 servings

Hints

This is easy and looks lovely.

Dee says you can use reduced-fat cream cheese and dessert topping: "No worries!"

Rockwell

Meredith Sifford

Meredith Sifford remembers the time she and her brother were supposed to keep an eye on the bread dough. Their mom asked them to make sure it didn't rise too much.

"We forgot," Meredith says with a grin. "By the time we remembered, the dough had risen out of the bowl and was all over the floor!"

Such a mishap might deter other bakers. But not Meredith. The 16-year-old blue ribbon winner has a spiritedness that shows in all her efforts. Active in her county's 4-H chapter for 10 years, she moved beyond local competitions to begin participating in the State Fair when she was only 12.

Meredith remembered the first time she entered. She wasn't even nervous. "We had gotten out of school early that day. My friends and I just went to enter our stuff and have fun."

Though they live a two-and-a-half-hour drive from Raleigh, Mary Ann and Terry Sifford feel participating in the Fair is important enough to make the trip each year. Their support and energy helped motivate their daughter, who in 1993, won seven blue ribbons.

Meredith's 4-H activities continue to play an important role in her life. As a junior leader, she takes part in "Summer Fling," a cooking class designed to introduce kids ages five through nine to basic cooking concepts. "We make cookies all day," Meredith says, "About 30 to 40 kids, making five different types of cookies in three ovens...then there's all the dishes to wash!"

In spite of her exuberance, this State Fair junior division winner takes her craft as seriously as her adult counterparts do. In addition to multiple baking categories, she enters canning and sewing. "Homemade bread is a lot of hard work," says Meredith, "and I don't make it very often. But I can make cakes that will rise up and be pretty."

"She's not heavy-handed," Meredith's mom adds. "Her grandmothers — and her great-grandmother, too — were good bakers."

Meredith has inherited that family legacy, giving her a sense of continuity and belonging. And if she needs help, both sets of her grandparents live just down the road.

It takes a lot of energy to compete, and Meredith Sifford's efforts have been recognized with ribbons, such as the one she received for this handmade dress.

Old Fashioned Cornbread
by Meredith Sifford

      2   cups self-rising cornmeal
      2   eggs
      2   cups cold milk
    1/2   cup melted margarine

Preheat oven to 425 degrees. Grease an 8x8" square pan and set aside.

Pour cornmeal into a mixing bowl. Add eggs, milk and melted margarine. Mix until well-blended. Pour into prepared pan and bake for 30

to 45 minutes, or until golden brown.
Remove from oven and cut into squares.
Yield: 8 to 12 servings

Hint
This is the traditional recipe made without sugar.

Easy No-Knead Bread or Rolls
by Meredith Sifford

2 3/4 cups warm water
4 teaspoons salt
2 packages dry yeast
8 cups flour + 1 teaspoon flour
3 eggs, beaten
1/2 cup oil
1/2 cup sugar

Grease 2 large or 3 small loaf pans. If you are making rolls, grease a baking sheet. Set aside.

In a small bowl, mix 3/4 cup warm water, 1 teaspoon salt, yeast and 1 teaspoon flour. Stir until blended. Set aside.

In a large bowl, combine 8 cups of flour, the remaining 3 teaspoons salt, eggs, oil, the remaining 2 cups warm water and sugar. Stir together.

Add yeast mixture to the flour mixture and stir until a sticky dough forms. Set aside, uncovered for 3 hours, stirring gently once every hour.

Punch down. Shape into loaves or rolls and place in prepared pans. Let rise for 1 hour.

While dough rises, preheat oven to 350 degrees. For bread, bake for 35 to 45 minutes. For rolls, bake 15 to 25 minutes or until golden brown.
Yield: 2 large loaves, 3 small loaves or about 3 dozen rolls

Hints
You can use half white and half wheat flour.

Don't forget about the dough during the 3 hours it rises — this is the recipe that rose out of the bowl onto Meredith's floor!

Kenly

Virginia Jackson

You can smell the biscuits through the screen door the moment you set foot on the front porch. Inside, Virginia Jackson's blue ribbon hangs above the mantel, right next to her family photographs and praying hands plaque.

The afternoon trains are passing through Kenly, and their whistles blow from just across the street where the tracks cut through town. Virginia sits to reminisce.

She grew up with tobacco and cotton, spending summers in the fields with her family. Thinking back to the days she worked alongside her father, Delie, she says, "The most cotton I ever picked was 150 pounds in one day. But even though he was in his 70s then, I still couldn't beat him. I made $100 for five or six weeks' work."

Given a choice, Virginia always preferred baking to picking cotton. She learned as a child.

"When my mother would get sick, she'd tell me how to make the biscuits — how much flour to put in, then lard, then milk," she says. "My brother used to tease me about them being hard."

Her mother, Lulah Richardson Hinnant, used what Virginia calls a "bread tray" to mix biscuits. The oval-shaped, shallow, wooden bowl always hung from a nail on the wall in their kitchen. One day the tray fell and cracked right down the center, but Delie put it back together with a piece of leather strap.

Virginia still uses that same bread tray every time she makes biscuits.

It was hard when Virginia's husband, James, died suddenly at age 45. She was left to raise their four boys by herself. But today she's happy just having Larry, Johnny, Randy and Rodney living nearby.

"Time is precious," she says.

None of Virginia's sons ever showed a knack for baking, but everyone near Kenly knows about Virginia's famous biscuits. She's baked thousands of them, four at a time in her own kitchen — and in batches of 800 at the Hardee's over in Smithfield.

Once, Virginia worked at a restaurant called Patrick's. The owner was concerned about cholesterol in the biscuits. Virginia told him, "Mr. Moore, I'm going to make them like you want, but they won't hold up."

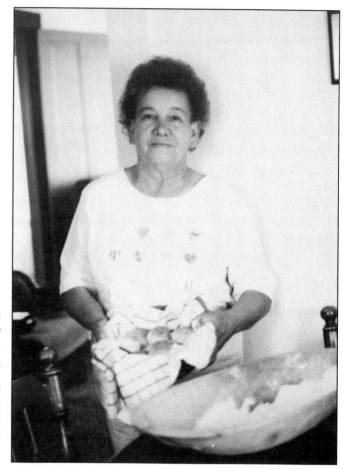

Virginia Jackson still makes her blue-ribbon-winning biscuits by hand, in this wooden "bread tray" that belonged to her mother.

She lightened up the recipe, then said, "Now, let me make some like I make at home.

"I sold him."

Good cooks often work without recipes, but the State Fair requires that you submit your recipe with each entry. Virginia didn't know about that rule when she decided, "I'll just bake some biscuits and carry them down there." They turned her away and she had to wait another year to enter and win.

Virginia can't remember all the contests she's won, but she never forgets the key to making perfect biscuits.

"Keep your mind on what you're doing; don't just throw them together," she advises.

And forget using a mixer or even a spoon; Virginia mixes every batch with her hands.

It seems so simple: three ingredients. So there must be a secret, something else that makes one biscuit — or cake or pie or bread — different and special. If that something else doesn't come from the store or out of a book, where does it come from? Can it be measured like so much flour and shortening?

In Virginia Jackson's strong, brown hands lies at least part of the secret. When your hands have worked the fields, tamed a garden and cared for children, almost anything is possible. Virginia's touch is unique. A talent like hers can be learned; it comes only by doing, with care and with practice. And learning takes time, an investment too few are willing to make. But there's something else still, something that comes from the heart.

Virginia remembers the time a neighbor tried to describe just what it was he liked so much about one of her biscuits. He thought about it a while, then decided it wasn't the color, the texture or even the taste.

"Virginia," he pronounced, "That biscuit's got 'tender loving care.'"

Buttermilk Biscuits
by Virginia Jackson

2   cups self-rising flour
1   tablespoon lard or shortening
3/4   cup buttermilk

Preheat oven to 500 degrees. Grease a baking sheet and set aside. Measure flour into a bowl. Make a well (or "hole") in the flour.
Add the shortening and buttermilk and mix together.
When the dough has lost some of its stickiness, "pinch" off a piece the size you want each biscuit to be. DO NOT ROLL OUT DOUGH. Pat each biscuit into shape and place on prepared baking sheet.
Bake until browned, 7 to 8 minutes for smaller biscuits, 9 to 10 minutes for larger biscuits.
Yield: 6 large or 8 small biscuits

Hints
Use your hands to mix the dough. You'll learn by feel when it's right. Lard helps hold the biscuits together, but shortening will work.

Virginia believes the less time the biscuit is in the oven, the better. Make sure your oven is hot enough.

About 2/3 of the way through cooking, use a spatula to lift one of the biscuits to check the browning underneath. If it's getting too brown, switch on the broiler for the rest of the cooking time, but WATCH CAREFULLY to avoid burning.

Cinnamon Raisin Biscuits
by Virginia Jackson

2	cups self-rising flour
3/4	teaspoon cinnamon
1/4	cup sugar
1	tablespoon lard or shortening
3/4	cup buttermilk
1/4-1/2	cup raisins

Preheat oven to 500 degrees. Grease a baking sheet and set aside.

Measure flour, cinnamon and sugar into a bowl. Make a well (or "hole") in the flour. Add the shortening and buttermilk and mix together. Add the raisins.

When the dough has lost some of its stickiness, "pinch" off a piece the size you want each biscuit to be. DO NOT ROLL OUT DOUGH. Pat each biscuit into shape and place on prepared baking sheet.

Bake until browned, 7 to 8 minutes for smaller biscuits, 9 to 10 minutes for larger biscuits.

Drizzle with your favorite icing, if desired.

Yield: 6 large or 8 small biscuits

Hints

Use your hands to mix the dough. You'll learn by feel when it's right.

Lard helps hold the biscuits together, but shortening will work.

Virginia believes the less time the biscuit is in the oven, the better. Make sure your oven is hot enough.

About 2/3 of the way through cooking, use a spatula to lift one of the biscuits to check the browning underneath. If it's getting too brown, switch on the broiler for the rest of the cooking time, but WATCH CAREFULLY to avoid burning.

A Final Note

"I'll never know how Mama got her biscuits so light."

"I wish I had my grandmother's recipe."

"No, they never wrote anything down when they cooked."

If there was any sadness about cooking in the hearts of the people I interviewed for this book, it came forth when they shared sentiments such as these. Good cooks usually can re-create a few of the favorite dishes they remember, but too often something hard to define is missing.

It should be so easy to set down a few lines on paper, to give our families this small link to the past that they can pass along to the next generation. But we're too busy. We don't think it matters, not compared to the other demands in our lives.

If you're the person who brings the pie at Thanksgiving or the cookies at Christmas, I urge you to share what you know with your friends and family. Write down your recipes. Tell the children and the grandchildren all the stories you remember about growing up on the farm or in the city or the old country.

Recipes are like snapshots from the best moments in life. Share them, treasure them and do everything you can to make sure they survive.

Index of Recipes

L

M

N

O

R

S

T

V

W

Y

Alphabetical Index
of Recipe Contributors

Adams, Linda
Alford, Joy
Barger, Emily
Bailey, Bobbie
Buie, Don and Becky
Carpenter, Linda
Caskey, Holly
Fishburne, Loring
Foust, Edna
Hall, Cheryl
Hamby, Ben
Hamby, Wendy
Hampton, Rose
Harris, Kris
Jackson, Virginia
Jones, Marie
Leverett, Carolyn
McLeod, Jennifer
McLeod, Margaret
Moser, Susan and Harvey
Pufpaff, Dee
Rayno, Cindy
Reitzel, Betty
Richardson, Mary
Seastrom, Lil
Sifford, Meredith
Vassello, Doug and Shari
Wolfe, Joanna